We would like to dedicate this book to our special family members who we lost over the past year.

Uncle Tim, who was very special to us. He was one of our favourite uncles and loved to cook too. He would tell all his friends about us and our cooking journey and get them to buy our books and support us. He was so proud of what we were doing, and we'll continue to make him proud in his memory. There's still no one that can better his coleslaw!

Aunty Angela, who was one of our biggest supporters. She always wanted the best for us, was always commenting on our posts, sending us messages of support and telling all her friends about us. She was so proud. We are going to miss having her around on Christmas day sharing a glass of Guinness punch. Aunty, we will continue to make you proud. RIP.

Our grandad Sydney, who was part of the Windrush generation and paved the way for most of our family to have a future in UK. Thank you for taking the decision to come to England. We will continue the legacy, we promise.

Also to our Nanny and grandad McAnuff. You are never forgotten. RIP.

NATURAL
FLAVA

CRAIG & SHAUN McANUFF

BLOOMSBURY PUBLISHING
LONDON · OXFORD · NEW YORK · NEW DELHI · SYDNEY

Introduction 7

GIVE THANKS 12
SNACKS & LIKKLE BITES 36
FEEL GOOD FLAVA 58
CURRIES & STEWS 96
FAMILY & SHARING FLAVA 130
FIRED UP FLAVA 160
SIDES, SALADS & SAUCES 188
SWEET ME NUH 216

Ingredients 242
Index 246
Acknowledgements 252

Introduction

Hey guys, we're back again with another cookbook! Wow. Our first one, *Original Flava*, was an amazing journey through our heritage, culture, food and family. We travelled to Jamaica in October 2018 to discover and celebrate Caribbean cooking at its source, and the array of delicious fresh produce the island has to offer, and now we have taken a different angle by using all the colourful and vibrant fruit and veg we found there to create *Natural Flava*. We started to explore and create exciting plant-based recipes because we wanted a healthier, more balanced diet, but we also want to show the world that there's more to Caribbean cooking than just jerk chicken. This book is packed with Caribbean-inspired plant-based recipes that are full of FLAVA.

Our trip to Jamaica was a life-changing experience, and it opened our eyes to cooking in a different way. We were exposed to Ital food, derived from Rastafarian culture, and this was a big influence on our journey into the plant-based lifestyle. Rastafarians believe that food should be eaten from the Earth, and to stay healthy and spiritually connected to the Earth, Rastas eat a natural diet that is free from additives and chemicals. This style of primarily vegan eating is known as Ital cooking – 'Ital is Vital' is often used to promote it. With this book, we are paying homage to Rastafarianism, which pioneers plant-based food and promotes a healthy mind, body, spirit and environment ethos.

On our trip, we visited vegan cafés in Negril and were amazed by how much natural food was so flavaful and delicious. We remember stopping at the café on Seven Mile Beach and ordering a meal which consisted of stew peas, curry tofu, rice and peas and cabbage; it tasted amazing – fresh and filling – and was truly one of the best meals we had. We realised that Jamaica was filled with delicious plant-based recipes that could be combined to create one meal.

We had started to get serious about making plant-based recipes when Shaun adopted a vegan diet for a year, back in 2018. While he was actively researching and living it, posting his meals on social media and creating amazing natural dishes, he was also seeing all the health benefits, including healthier skin and weight loss. Craig was then inspired to begin experimenting with plant-based foods too, and found he loved it. The Caribbean is rightly celebrated for its curry goat, chicken and fish dishes, but we wanted to be innovative and create new Caribbean dishes using all the natural ingredients we ate and cooked with during our stay in Jamaica.

In Afro-Caribbean culture, where traditional food is high in fats and carbs, people have a much higher risk of developing diabetes and high blood pressure, which are among the leading causes of death; consuming too much meat and dairy on a regular basis is a major factor, and has long-term implications for overall health. This informed our drive to find a healthy balance, and we want to inspire our culture and help more people, especially Afro-Caribbean people, consume a more plant-based diet. Our mother and older brother were also motivated and started to adopt a more plant-based lifestyle, and have now become vegans! Our mum previously had type 2 diabetes and high blood pressure, which she now manages through her healthy diet. However, we are in no way demanding that you become a vegan or be militant about it, and this cookbook is not just for vegans or plant-based eaters. This book is for everyone! No matter what diet you follow – meat-eater, fish-eater – we are sure you'll find recipes you'll love for yourself, friends and family. You will enjoy the FLAVA!

Food is something that is really big in our family; it is what brings us all together at family functions. Our nanny and mum inspired us to start cooking because of their passion for it and, being so close to them, we wanted to do it too. Our nanny plays a massive part in our business, and our followers love her as though she was their own nan. We introduced her to plant-based foods three years ago and at first she couldn't really see why we would make so many vegan recipes – she thought being vegan was some type of religion, lol. But as time went on she grew to understand it; she loved the healthier aspect and couldn't believe how delicious the food was. Our mum is also a massive support to us. She was always in the kitchen when we were growing up, like it was her second home. Providing meals day in, day out – we really respected it and wanted to support her any way we could, because our dad didn't cook much.

Growing up in a Caribbean household, we don't remember having too many vegetables on our plate, but now we use vegetables in a way we never thought we could. I mean, plantain and chickpea curry, jerk-spiced squash and callaloo Wellington and mushroom pepper steak! We are all about making these foods exciting and attractive, and appealing to a wider audience. We want to inspire people to eat more plants, even if it's once or twice a week – small changes can lead you towards a more balanced diet in the long run. We have found a formula that involves giving plant-based food the same treatment as meat or fish to create dishes with maximum flava, transferring traditional Caribbean methods to plant-based foods; it's all about the seasoning and preparation. For example, the staple Caribbean dish of brown stew chicken is transformed into brown stew broccoli. Vegetables absorb flavour so well, creating a delicious taste like no other.

We are both fathers now, which is the biggest blessing of all time. Craig has twin girls, and Shaun has a son, and they are growing so fast! With only three months between them, they are able to grow together just like we did. Being fathers has given us a bigger responsibility to be role models to our kids and an even bigger passion to leave a legacy for them to be proud of. Food is such an important part of children's development, making sure they get the right nutrients and vitamins in their bodies. Our knowledge and understanding of plant-based recipes has really helped us in feeding our kids and providing daily meals. As soon as they could eat solids, we would make fresh food daily, blending things like sweet potatoes, butternut squash, plantains, yam and callaloo to a paste. As they got a bit older we introduced them to more of the food we were eating, just not the spicy parts. Craig's daddy duties have even included making natural hair formulas every week for his twins, using avocado and oils to promote healthy hair.

Through our social media, we have inspired many people to eat more of a plant-based diet, and many of our followers have asked us for a physical vegan book: here with *Natural Flava* we have finally made it happen. We have explored the natural flavours of the Caribbean to create imaginative, original dishes that not only taste great but are accessible to everyone. Prepare to be belly-full with tantalising FLAVA!

— Craig & Shaun

Give Thanks   14

From a young age, we were often woken in the mornings by the most incredible smells! Giving thanks for a new day is made better with some great food, and even now we still look forward to it as much as we did then.

Whether it was Mum's cooked-down ackee, the sizzling, fragrant fried dumpling oil or Nan's nutmeg-infused cornmeal porridge, we knew we'd always be in for a treat!

This chapter is all about bringing that excitement to your mornings – food you dream about waking up to, and nutritious drinks that will boost not just your immune system, but your taste buds too!

You'll find a great mix of recipes here, from plant-based milks made from scratch, comforting porridges and thick, filling smoothies using the best and most exotic ingredients, to pancakes and heartier savoury dishes of muffins and dumplings. They will all have you singing like those three likkle birdies Bob was talking 'bout!

Give Thanks   17

Coconut pancakes with warm blueberries

Mmmmm, these taste so, so good! Coconut has a lovely flavour and together with the warm berry compote is a match made in sweet heaven!

Also, if you prefer other berries to blueberries, use them instead – cook down, dash dem pon top of the pancakes and enjoy!

First, toast the desiccated coconut in a frying pan until golden. Mix the toasted coconut, flour, sugar, baking powder, flaxseed and salt together in a bowl. In a separate jug or bowl, mix the coconut milk, water, vanilla and melted butter together and combine well, then add to the dry ingredients and mix together to create a sloppy consistency.

In the frying pan, heat some coconut oil over a high heat. Use a large spoon and drop the mixture into the pan then lower the heat to medium and cook for a few minutes, until bubbles start to appear in the centre. Flip over and cook the other side until golden brown. Repeat with the rest of the mixture. Keep the pancakes warm while you make the compote.

Cook the frozen blueberries down in a small pan with a sprinkling of icing sugar until warmed through. Serve on top of the pancakes, then scatter on some toasted coconut flakes, if you like.

30g desiccated coconut
200g self-raising flour
½ tbsp brown sugar
1 tsp baking powder
1 tbsp ground flaxseed
Pinch of salt
200ml coconut milk
140ml water
1 tsp vanilla extract
½ tbsp unsalted vegan butter, melted, or oil
Coconut oil, for frying
200g frozen blueberries
Sprinkling of icing sugar
Coconut flakes, toasted, to serve (optional)

Hard-dough French toast with tropical fruits

Serves 2–3

Sweet with a hint of spice and some tropical fruits! Start your weekend off with a bang and try this delicious recipe! Hard-dough bread is a popular sweet bread eaten throughout the Caribbean, and we've created a likkle French toast flava with exotic fruits and spices.

Put the milk into a shallow rectangular bowl, add the cinnamon, nutmeg, sugar, vanilla and melted butter, then mix together.

Heat a likkle oil in a large frying pan over a medium-high heat. Dunk your bread slices into the milk mixture on both sides, then fry for 1–2 minutes on each side until golden brown.

Top with the fruit and drizzle with syrup to serve.

250ml plant-based milk of your choice
1 tsp ground cinnamon
1 tsp freshly grated nutmeg
2 tbsp brown sugar
1 tsp vanilla extract
2 tbsp vegan butter, melted
Olive oil, for frying
6 slices of hard-dough bread (ensure vegan), about 2cm thick
A selection of prepared tropical fruits, such as papaya, mango, passionfruit, pineapple, banana
Golden syrup, for drizzling

Give Thanks

Ital breakfast platter

Serves 4

The taste of Ital all in one breakfast! This one is a treat for the weekend. Sweet hard-dough bread in a French-toast style, topped with ackee and callaloo. WOW, this is making me hungry just thinking about it. The flava of sweet, savoury and spice will put you in a good mood for the rest of the day. Share with the family and the kids too.

Heat a likkle oil in a frying pan over a medium heat, add the onion, garlic and scotch bonnet and cook down for 5 minutes until soft. Add the tomatoes, then the callaloo, and mix together. Season with black pepper and cook for 5–7 minutes, then remove from the pan and keep warm.

In the same pan, add the ackee, butter, thyme and black pepper to taste, mix together and simmer for 5 minutes. Remove from the pan and keep warm.

Add the mushrooms to the same pan and cook down until soft, season with black pepper and simmer to evaporate their liquid and caramelise them. Remove from the pan and keep warm.

For the French toast, add the coconut milk, sugar, vanilla and cinnamon to a medium bowl and whisk until smooth. Heat a likkle coconut oil a frying pan over a medium-high heat. Dip the bread slices into the liquid mixture then add to the hot oil and cook for 1–2 minutes on each side until golden brown. Transfer to a plate lined with kitchen paper.

Add a likkle more coconut oil to the frying pan and fry the plantain slices for 1–2 minutes on each side.

Plate up by placing the ackee, callaloo, mushrooms and plantain on top of the French toast, then drizzle over golden syrup. Serve with the avocado, if you like, on the side.

Coconut oil, for frying
1 medium onion, diced
4 garlic cloves, finely chopped
1 scotch bonnet pepper, deseeded
  and diced
2 tomatoes, chopped
1 x 280g can callaloo, drained
1 x 540g can ackee, drained
1 tbsp vegan butter
½ tsp dried thyme
200g chestnut mushrooms, sliced
2 ripe plantain, peeled and sliced
Golden syrup, for drizzling
1 avocado, peeled, stoned
  and sliced (optional)
Freshly ground black pepper

For the French toast
1 x 400ml can coconut milk
1 tsp brown sugar
1 tsp vanilla extract
1 tsp ground cinnamon
4 thick slices of hard-dough bread
  (ensure vegan)

Caribbean breakfast muffin

Serves 4

Breakfast muffin sandwich just got a Caribbean makeover. Once you have tried this muffin, you won't look at another the same again! Sandwiched together with a fried dumpling top and bottom, it's honestly drool-worthy!

We usually have these muffins (as it says in the title) for breakfast, but we also have them whenever we crave them. And they hit the spot every time!

Mix the flour, salt and melted butter in a bowl, then gradually add enough water to bring it together into a dough. Knead until smooth, then cover and set aside in the fridge for 10 minutes to rest.

Meanwhile, heat a likkle vegetable oil in a frying pan over a medium heat, add the onion, garlic and bell pepper and cook down for about 5 minutes until soft, then add the callaloo and cook for 5 minutes. Add the ackee, black pepper and thyme, mix together and simmer for another 5 minutes. Remove from the heat and keep warm.

Heat a likkle oil in a separate frying pan over a medium heat, add the plantain and fry for 1–2 minutes on each side, until golden brown. Remove from the pan and keep warm.

Add enough oil to the pan for shallow-frying and heat over a medium heat. Remove the dumpling dough from the fridge, divide into 4 equal pieces and shape each into a muffin, about 8cm in diameter. Fry for 3–4 minutes each side until golden brown, then remove to a plate lined with kitchen paper and leave to cool and drain.

To assemble the breakfast muffin, split your dumplings in half crossways. Add the ackee and callaloo to the base and top with plantain. Drizzle with jerk BBQ sauce or ketchup, put the other muffin half on top and nyam!

200g self-raising flour
1 tsp salt
1 tbsp vegan butter, melted
About 120ml water
Vegetable oil, for frying
1 small onion, chopped
2 garlic cloves, chopped
½ red bell pepper, deseeded and chopped
1 x 280g can callaloo, drained
1 x 280g can ackee, drained
1 tsp freshly ground black pepper
1 tsp dried thyme
1–2 ripe plantain, peeled and sliced
Jerk BBQ sauce (see page 166 for homemade) or ketchup, to serve

Give Thanks   27

Ackee and cabbage with fried dumplings and plantain

Serves 2–3

This recipe is inspired by Jamaica's national dish ackee and saltfish, but we've replaced the saltfish for white cabbage. Cooked down, cabbage has a lovely silky texture with a soft crunch and is the perfect complement for ackee.

We've added fried wholemeal dumplings and plantain to make this a breakfast or brunch that you'll keep coming back to over and over again.

For the dumplings, mix the flour, baking powder, salt and melted butter in a bowl, then gradually add enough water to bring it together into a dough. Knead until smooth, then cover and set aside in the fridge for 10 minutes to rest.

Meanwhile, heat the 2 tablespoons of coconut oil in a frying pan over a medium heat, add the onion, garlic and spring onions and cook for about 10 minutes until softened. Add the tomato and bell peppers and cook down until soft. Dash in the cabbage, give it a stir and cook down until nearly soft, then season di ting with some salt and black pepper, the pimento, thyme and scotch bonnet and mix together. Add the ackee and stir it in gently, then simmer for 5 minutes. Keep warm while you fry the dumplings and plantain.

Remove the dumpling dough from the fridge. Pull off a golfball-sized piece and roll into a ball using the palms of your hands. Use your thumb to make a dimple in the middle, and repeat the process with the remaining dough. Heat enough coconut oil for shallow-frying in a separate frying pan and fry the dumplings, dimple side down first, over a medium heat for 3–4 minutes on each side until golden brown. Remove to a plate lined with kitchen paper to drain.

Add a likkle more oil to the pan, if needed, and shallow-fry the plantain slices for 1–2 minutes each side until golden brown. Serve the ackee and cabbage, dumplings and plantain with the wilted spinach.

2 tbsp coconut oil
1 medium onion, diced
4 garlic cloves, finely chopped
2 spring onions, chopped
1 large tomato, chopped
½ red bell pepper, deseeded and cut into strips
½ green bell pepper, deseeded and cut into strips
300g white cabbage, shredded
1 tsp ground pimento (allspice)
2–3 fresh thyme sprigs
1 scotch bonnet pepper, deseeded and chopped
1 x 540g can ackee, drained
75g fresh spinach, wilted, to serve
Salt and coarsely ground black pepper

For the dumplings and plantain
375g plain wholemeal flour
1 tsp baking powder
Pinch of salt
1 tsp vegan butter, melted
About 225ml water
Coconut oil, for shallow-frying
2 ripe plantain, peeled and sliced

Give Thanks

Vegan milks

Here's a couple of natural plant-based milks made from scratch that are a little different to the almond and oat milks we also enjoy.

Coconut milk is a fundamental aspect of vegan cooking; it is so versatile and we use it a lot – from curries, to soups and sweet treats!

Plantain milk

Makes 1 litre

2 ripe plantain, peeled and sliced
2 dates, stoned
1 litre water
Squeeze of lime juice
Salt

Add the sliced plantain to a blender with the dates and water and blend until smooth.

Use a milk bag, or a sieve lined with a cheesecloth set over a bowl, and filter the milk through. Season with lime juice and salt to taste. Store in a sealed glass jar or bottle in the fridge for up to 5 days.

Fresh coconut milk

Makes 500ml

1 whole coconut, or 700g fresh coconut pieces
180ml water

If using a whole coconut, the easiest way to break open is to fling it on a hard floor as hard as you can – but it's not the most careful way! A more sensible way would be to first locate one of the three 'eyes' near the stem, push a screwdriver through it and pour out the liquid. Then use the back of a chef's knife to knock one part of the coconut repeatedly until it cracks open. Gouge the flesh out using a small, sharp knife and cut into pieces.

Dash the coconut pieces into a blender and pour in the water; it should come halfway up the level of the coconut. Blitz until smooth as it can be.

Strain through a sieve lined with a cheesecloth and placed over a bowl, pressing down on it using a spatula to release the juice.

That's it, you've just made coconut milk. Store in a sealed glass jar or bottle in the fridge for up to 2 weeks.

Warm-spiced cornmeal porridge   Serves 4

A real breakfast favourite for us growing up. We stayed at our nan's house a lot and used to really look forward to eating this comforting and warming porridge in the morning. Even at our older age we ask Nan to make it for us when we come round! It's that good!

Fine cornmeal expands into a thick porridge and is flava'd up with cinnamon and nutmeg and sweetened with coconut or plant-based condensed milk. Yum yum!

Add 600ml of the oat milk and the coconut milk to a saucepan with the cinnamon and nutmeg and bring to the boil over a low heat.

Just before the milk boils, add the cornmeal to a mixing bowl and stir in the remaining 300ml oat milk to make a smooth mixture. Add to the pan of boiling milk and use a whisk to mix until smooth. Add the vanilla and salt, then sweeten to taste with condensed milk. Continue to cook over a low heat, stirring, until thickened.

Serve with sugar or golden syrup for extra sweetness, if you like.

900ml oat milk
200ml coconut milk
1 cinnamon stick (halved if long)
  or ¼ tsp ground cinnamon
½ tsp freshly grated nutmeg
200g fine cornmeal
1 tbsp vanilla extract
Pinch of salt, or to taste
Sweetened condensed coconut
  milk or vegan milk, to taste
Sugar or golden syrup, to serve
  (optional)

Ital smoothies

Four flavalicious smoothies that taste great and are good fi yuh! Each beneficial in a different way.

Place handfuls of ice in a blender, then all the ingredients for your chosen smoothie. Blitz until smooth.

Boost

125g peeled mango, cut into chunks
125g peeled and cored pineapple, cut into chunks
1 banana, peeled and cut into chunks
2.5cm piece of fresh ginger, peeled
50ml coconut water
2 tbsp golden syrup

Immune

50g spinach
2 bananas, peeled and cut into chunks
½ cucumber, cut into chunks
1 tbsp spirulina
20g pumpkin seeds
450ml coconut water

Detox

1 cucumber, cut into chunks
200g peeled watermelon, cut into chunks
1 tbsp chia seeds
1 kiwi, peeled
Squeeze of lime juice
100ml water

Glow

2 carrots, chopped
1 tsp ground turmeric
½ pineapple
5cm piece of fresh ginger, peeled
1 apple, cored
60ml pineapple juice
200ml water

Give Thanks

Crunchy tropical granola

This homemade tropical granola is full of flavas from the Caribbean! It's quick and easy to make so will save you a lot of time in the mornings – a great way to get your daily fruits in using the most tropical fruit you can find, finished off with a crunch to wake you up.

Preheat the oven to 140°C Fan/160°C/Gas 3.

Add the oil, syrup and vanilla to a saucepan and stir over a medium heat until combined. Stir in the remaining ingredients to coat completely, then spread the mixture out on a large baking sheet (you may need two, or to bake this in two batches). Bake in the oven for 30–35 minutes until golden brown, stirring it well halfway through.

Stored in an airtight container, this will keep for up to 3 days.

2 tbsp extra virgin olive oil
50g golden syrup
1 tsp vanilla extract
250g jumbo oats
Pinch of salt
100g whole almonds
75g plantain chips
75g dried papaya
75g dried mango
75g fresh coconut pieces
Pinch of salt

Mint tea

Serves 2

Our mum and nan love their herbal teas. We've definitely taken on their love for them, and we like to create them from scratch, too. Nothing better than a fusion of fresh ingredients to help settle your mind and body, and warm ya belly too.

Often used as an easy way to get natural detoxifying ingredients into your diet, homemade teas are common in a Caribbean household. There's something enjoyable about knowing you've made a fresh herbal tea yourself, and we find the premade sort in bags a little bitter. So these teas offer a lovely balance of health and enjoyment to your teas.

500ml water (filtered)
15 fresh mint leaves (peppermint or spearmint)
1 tsp grated fresh ginger
2 slices of lemon
Golden syrup, to taste

Bring the water to the boil in a saucepan. Add the mint leaves then turn down to a low-medium heat.

Add the grated ginger and lemon slices and simmer for 10–15 minutes. Sweeten to taste with golden syrup.

Lemongrass tea

Serves 2

Aka 'fever grass tea' in the Caribbean, where it's known as a remedy for fevers and, according to Nan, any fever in ah yuh, it gwan after you sip dis! And to be honest it's always worked for us!

Lemongrass is widely grown in Jamaica, and we saw lots of it in our uncle's herb garden – it's full of health benefits, such as helping to relieve bloating, and is actually very relaxing for the mind too!

500ml water (filtered)
2 lemongrass stalks
2 slices of lemon
Golden syrup, to taste

Bring the water to the boil in a saucepan.

Bash the lemongrass stalks with a cup to release their flavour, add them to the pan then turn down to a low-medium heat.

Add the lemon slices and leave to simmer for 10–15 minutes. Sweeten to taste with golden syrup.

SNACKS

&

LIKKLE BITES

Snacks and Likkle Bites

If you're looking for something easy to eat on the go, or for a quick lunch, this is the chapter for you. We've got small bites packed with BIG flavas: plantain hummus, callaloo fritters and vegan patties. We've even got a spicy vegan fried 'chicken' recipe. YES! Read that again, we've got one and it's banging! The tastiest plant-based fried chicken recipe you'll ever find.

These likkle plates pack a mighty punch. As Jamaicans say, 'likkle but tallawah', which means we may be small but we are strong! In other words, we might call these snacks, but they also do the trick to fill you in the right places.

Snacks and Likkle Bites   40

Plantain hummus

We've created some Mediterranean-Caribbean FLAVA with this quick and easy plantain hummus that everyone will enjoy. Thick, creamy and sweet, but with a peppery kick.

Cook the plantain in a pan of boiling water for 12–15 minutes until tender, then drain and refresh in cold water to cool it down.

Add to a food processor or a blender with the remaining ingredients except the hot pepper sauce, and blend for about 3 minutes until smooth, adding some water if the hummus is too thick. Transfer to a serving bowl, drizzle a little olive oil and hot pepper sauce on top and serve with pitta bread, hard-dough bread and/or raw veggies.

Store in the fridge for up to 5 days.

2 ripe plantain, peeled and cut into chunks
1 x 400g can chickpeas, drained and rinsed
2 tbsp tahini
60ml olive oil, plus extra for serving
4 garlic cloves, chopped
1 scotch bonnet pepper, deseeded and chopped
Juice of ½ lemon
1 tsp salt
Pinch of freshly ground black pepper
Hot pepper sauce, to serve

Snacks and Likkle Bites 43

Stew pea dumpling taco

Serves 4
or 8 as a side

Tacos just got a Caribbean makeover, Original Flava style! Tacos are definitely one of those feel-good meals to enjoy, but with this mouth-drooling Caribbean-inspired version you'll be bussin' a salsa dance and gully creep at the same time.

We've included a stew peas filling, which is cooked-down kidney beans that create the most incredibly rich sauce, and we've taken the dough recipe for traditional Jamaican dumplings to create the taco wrap. It's a match made in heaven. You'll love this!

Start with the dumpling tacos. Add the flour, baking powder, salt, butter and water to a large mixing bowl and mix together to combine into a dough. Knead until smooth, adding more water if it seems too dry, or more flour if it is too sticky. Shape into a ball, wrap in cling film and rest in the fridge for 15 minutes.

Heat a likkle oil in a large frying pan over a medium heat, then add the onion and garlic and cook down for 5–7 minutes until soft. Add the kidney beans with the liquid from the cans, along with the coconut milk, thyme and 1 teaspoon of black pepper, and cook for 15 minutes over a low heat until the liquid has evaporated.

In a small bowl, mix the diced avocado, tomato and scotch bonnet, season with lemon juice, salt and black pepper, and set aside.

For the dumpling tacos, lightly dust your work surface with flour and remove the rested dough from the fridge. Cut into 8 equal pieces, then use a rolling pin to roll out each into circles about 10cm in diameter.

Heat 4 tablespoons of vegetable oil in a frying pan over a high heat, add the taco dough circles (you may need to do this in batches), turn the heat down to medium and cook for 3–4 minutes until golden brown and lightly blistered on each side. Remove to a plate lined with kitchen paper to drain.

Score a line down the middle of each taco, and carefully fold. Serve filled with the stew peas and avocado mixture, with mayo and chilli sauce on the side, garnished with parsley leaves.

400g plain flour, plus extra
    for dusting
1 tsp baking powder
1 tsp salt
1 tsp vegan butter
225ml water
Vegetable oil, for frying
1 avocado, peeled, stoned and diced
1 large tomato, diced
¼ scotch bonnet pepper, deseeded
    and diced
Squeeze of lemon juice
Salt and freshly ground black
    pepper

For the stew peas
1 onion, diced
4 garlic cloves, chopped
2 x 400g cans kidney beans
    (don't drain)
200ml coconut milk
1 tsp dried thyme

To serve
Vegan mayo
Sweet chilli sauce
Handful of parsley leaves

Caribbean-spiced jackfruit wraps with plum sauce

Serves 4

Someone say Friday night flava! Yup, this is a weekend fave for us. We like to switch it up sometimes depending on our mood, adding extra sauce toppings and extra spice if we feeling nice! Lawd ah mercy this wrap will defo pull the right strings – give it a go! Jeez!

First, let's start with the jackfruit. Shred the pieces with your hands and place in a mixing bowl. Now let's season di ting! Add the cumin, thyme, paprika, pimento, cinnamon and a likkle salt and black pepper. Stir to coat, then set aside for 15 minutes to marinate.

Meanwhile, make the plum sauce. Add all the ingredients to a small pan and simmer for about 10 minutes until thick and the plums are fully broken down. Add salt to taste and keep warm.

Heat 1 tablespoon of oil in a frying pan, add the onion, ginger and scotch bonnet and cook over a medium heat for 5 minutes until soft, then add in the seasoned jackfruit and cook, stirring occasionally, for 8–10 minutes until the edges of the jackfruit have crisped slightly.

Now, it's time to build the wraps. Lay out each tortilla and add a layer of jackfruit, cucumber slices, spring onion and carrot. And a generous dollop of plum sauce. If ya bad, add some pepper sauce on top too! Wrap together and enjoy da flava!

2 x 400g cans young green jackfruit in brine, drained and rinsed
1 tsp ground cumin
1 tsp dried thyme
1 tsp paprika
1 tsp ground pimento (allspice)
1 tsp ground cinnamon
Vegetable oil, for cooking
1 onion, thinly sliced
2cm piece of fresh ginger, grated
½ scotch bonnet pepper, deseeded
Salt and freshly ground black pepper

For the plum sauce
3 plums, stoned and diced
1 tsp paprika
1 tsp ground cumin
1 tsp ground pimento (allspice)
1 tsp ground cinnamon
1 tsp dried thyme
6cm piece of fresh ginger, grated
100ml hoisin sauce
50ml dark soy sauce
2 tsp golden syrup
1 tbsp white sugar
60ml apple cider vinegar

To assemble and serve
8 small (or 4 large) tortilla wraps, warmed
½ cucumber, thinly sliced
2 spring onions, thinly sliced
1 carrot, cut into julienne
Pepper sauce (optional)

Callaloo fritters

Fritters are a popular snack eaten throughout the Caribbean, and are loved by all. This recipe is fresh and light, using callaloo, the Caribbean's green leafy version of spinach, and packed full of nutrients. The perfect on-the-go bite!

You just can't go wrong with these! So, soo good!

Heat 2 tablespoons of oil in a frying pan over a high heat, add the onion, garlic and bell peppers and sauté for 3 minutes. Add the paprika, ginger and thyme, then stir in the callaloo and mix together. Add the scotch bonnet and tomato, with salt and pepper to taste. Cook for 5 minutes until the tomato softens into the callaloo. Set aside.

Sift the flour and baking powder into a bowl, add the callaloo mixture along with the water and mix together into a batter.

Heat enough oil for shallow-frying in a clean frying pan over a medium heat, add large spoonfuls of the batter and fry for 4–5 minutes on each side until golden brown.

Remove to a plate lined with kitchen paper, to absorb excess oil, and repeat until all the batter has been used up.

Vegetable oil, for frying
1 medium onion, diced
2 garlic cloves, finely chopped
½ red bell pepper, deseeded and diced
½ green bell pepper, deseeded and diced
½ yellow bell pepper, deseeded and diced
2 tsp paprika
1 tsp ground ginger
2 tsp dried thyme
1 x 540g can callaloo, lightly drained
1 scotch bonnet pepper, deseeded and finely chopped
1 tomato, chopped
300g plain flour
1 tsp baking powder
150ml water
Salt and freshly ground black pepper

Callaloo patties

Makes 6

Where do we start with these? WOW: FLAVA all over it, in ah' it and all around it. The patty, a turmeric-spiced buttery pastry, is one of the most loved savoury treats to come out of the Caribbean. It is known for its various filling options, and we love it with callaloo. Give this a go and share with your friends and fam.

Start with the pastry. Add the flour, turmeric, curry powder and a big pinch of salt to a large mixing bowl, and mix to combine. Add the butter and lard and rub into the flour with your fingertips until crumbly and there are no lumps. Add the water and mix to combine into a dough. Knead briefly into a large ball, wrap in cling film and chill in the fridge or freezer for 15 minutes.

Preheat the oven to 180°C Fan/200°C/Gas 6.

Heat the oil in a large frying pan over a medium heat, add the onion, garlic and scotch bonnet and cook down for a few minutes. Add the callaloo and pimento, season with salt and black pepper to taste and cook, stirring, for 5–7 minutes. Take off the heat and allow to cool.

Take the chilled dough out of the fridge. Dust the work surface with some flour to prevent the dough from sticking and cut the dough into 6 equal pieces. Roll out each piece using a rolling pin into a circle, just over 16cm in diameter.

Place an upturned bowl, about 16cm in diameter, on the dough round and cut around it using a sharp knife. Repeat with the remaining dough to make 6 rounds.

Spoon equal amounts of the cooled callaloo filling in the centre of each pastry circle, brush the edges with a likkle water to help them stick, then fold over to make semi-circles, using your fingers to seal the edges together. Use a fork to press around the edge to secure the join and crimp, then use a fork to poke a few rows of steam holes in the centre of each patty.

Place on a baking tray and bake in the oven for 25 minutes until cooked and golden.

1 tbsp vegetable oil
1 white onion, diced
4 garlic cloves, finely chopped
1 scotch bonnet pepper, deseeded and diced
1 x 540g can callaloo, drained
1 tsp ground pimento (allspice)
Salt and freshly ground black pepper

For the pastry

400g self-raising flour, plus extra for dusting
1 tsp ground turmeric
1 tsp curry powder
80g cold vegan butter, cut into small cubes
100g cold plant-based lard or shortening, cut into small cubes
6 tbsp cold water

Corn fritters

We love a fritter – the crunchy textures, intense flavours and spicy kick make it one of most enjoyable go-tos! These corn ones are so indulgent you could easily eat them all in one go... so make sure you make enough for you to sneak one in ahead of everyone else, and just enough for them to enjoy too! Once they hit the dining table, they'll be gone in a flash!

We recommend a tamarind sauce for dipping, but our mango chilli sauce on page 215 is also delicious. The sweetness is a great complement to the spices in the fritters.

Preheat the oven to 180°C Fan/200°C/Gas 6.

Heat the coconut oil in a frying pan over a medium heat, then add the onion, garlic, scotch bonnet, spring onions and parsley, and cook down for 5–7 minutes until caramelised. Set aside.

In a large mixing bowl, add the sweetcorn, flour, paprika, salt and black pepper. Stir in the caramelised veg, add the milk and melted butter and mix together into a thick batter.

Half-fill a large, deep, heavy pan with vegetable oil and place over a high heat. Heat to 160°C – to test if the oil is hot enough, drop in a piece of bread; if it turns golden in 30 seconds, it's ready. In small batches, use an ice-cream scoop or a medium-sized spoon to add fritters to the hot oil. Fry for 3–4 minutes until golden brown, then transfer to a baking tray and finish in the oven for 10–15 minutes.

Serve with tamarind sauce, mango chilli jam or any other dipping sauce.

1 tsp coconut oil
1 small onion, diced
2 garlic cloves, chopped
1 scotch bonnet pepper, deseeded and finely chopped
2 spring onions, sliced
20g parsley, finely chopped
1 x 340g can sweetcorn, drained
275g self-raising flour
1 tsp paprika
1 tsp salt
1 tsp coarsely ground black pepper
250ml plant-based milk of your choice
1 tbsp vegan butter, melted
Vegetable oil, for deep-frying
Tamarind sauce, for dipping (or another dipping sauce of your choice)

Snacks and Likkle Bites   55

Spicy fried 'chicken'

Serves 4

We were around so many fast food chicken shops when we were growing up. They were everywhere, and even though they were delicious it wasn't always the best food for you...

Banana blossom is a fleshy purple-skinned flower that has a similar texture to meat. It's an alkaline food with many benefits and the perfect veggie to fry like chicken. The big difference is – it's not chicken!

Preheat the oven to 180°C Fan/200°C/Gas 6.

Add the salt, black pepper, paprika, chilli powder, pimento, thyme, garlic and coconut milk to a mixing bowl and stir together to mix. In a separate bowl, combine the flour, baking powder, cornflour and curry powder.

Drain and rinse the banana blossom, then squeeze out any excess moisture and pat dry with kitchen paper.

Half-fill a large, deep, heavy pan with vegetable oil and place over a high heat. Heat to 160°C – to test if the oil is hot enough, drop in a piece of bread; if it turns golden in 30 seconds, it's ready. (Alternatively, you can shallow-fry these.)

Dip the banana blossom into the liquid mixture, then into the flour mixture and repeat (double dip for extra crunch). Deep-fry for 5 minutes until golden brown, transfer to a baking tray and finish in the oven for 10 minutes.

Meanwhile, put a large pan of water on to boil. Wash the potatoes and cut into fries (skin on). Boil the potatoes for 5 minutes then drain, pat dry and deep-fry in batches in the hot oil until cooked and dark golden. Toss with the mixed herbs and a likkle salt while still hot.

1 tsp sea salt, plus extra for the fries
1 tsp freshly ground black pepper
1 tsp paprika
1 tsp chilli powder
1 tsp ground pimento (allspice)
1 tsp dried thyme
2 garlic cloves, very finely chopped
200ml coconut milk
250g plain flour
1 tsp baking powder
1 tbsp cornflour
1 tbsp curry powder
1 x 520g can banana blossom
Vegetable oil, for deep-frying
4 large potatoes, washed and cut into fries (skin on)
1 tbsp dried mixed herbs

OOD

FLAVA

We've created this chapter especially for those who are after not just easy midweek comfort, but weekend dishes to indulge in after a long week. Introducing you to... vegan FLAVA to the MAX! Fried cauliflower burger and crunchy slaw filling, fried dumpling pizza, sweet and sour tofu... and much more.

We want people to know that you can fully indulge in those vegan food moments, whether it's a fakeaway at home, or an easy midweek pasta pick-me-up.

BIG FLAVOURS, crunchy textures, creamy sauces – we've got plenty for you to enjoy here, to give you that feel-good flava!

Feel Good Flava   63

Flava bowls

When we were in Jamaica we'd have these most amazing meals, filled with so much vibrancy, colour and texture, it was like a carnival on the tongue. Without the rum punch, though! The food had so much fuel to it, great carbs and vegetables, producing the energy needed to enjoy the rest of the day. And that's what's in these bowls. A sight that will brighten your day and your stomachs too!

The great thing about them is that the ingredients are all accessible in the UK, so we can close our eyes and pretend we back ah yard! And if you can't get access to any, we've given alternatives you can use instead. You can also mix and match the fillings to use whatever you have in the fridge, or to liven up leftovers.

Here are four of our all-time favourite flava bowls.

Green banana, cornmeal dumplings, ackee, fried plantain, cabbage, callaloo

This is the ideal meal for a Rasta to be eating in the blue mountains of Jamaica! A mixture of hard food and delicious flava packed with protein, fibre and a whole heap of goodness that's nourishing and will keep you full and ready for the day. You're getting so many different flavas and textures in this bowl.

Green banana

1 green (unripe) banana (or ½ butternut squash, peeled and cut into 2cm chunks)
Salt

Wash the unpeeled banana and pat dry. Then cut off both ends and make a slit down the middle of the skin.

Add (unpeeled) to boiling, salted water and cook for 20 minutes until tender. Drain, then carefully peel off the skin, using tongs to hold the banana.

Cornmeal dumplings

125g plain flour
125g fine cornmeal
1 tsp salt
About 125ml water

Half-fill a large pot with water, add a likkle salt then bring to the boil.

Meanwhile, mix together the flour, cornmeal and salt in a bowl. Gradually add enough water to bring the ingredients together into a dough. Knead with your hands into a smooth ball.

Pinch off a piece of the dough, shape into a ball between your palms, then flatten. Repeat with the rest of the dough to make 4–6 dumplings and cook in the boiling water for 10 minutes until tender.

Ackee

2 tbsp coconut oil
1 small onion, chopped
2 garlic cloves, finely chopped
1 red bell pepper, deseeded and chopped
1 large tomato, chopped
2 fresh thyme sprigs
1 tsp freshly ground black pepper
1 tsp paprika
1 x 540g can ackee

Heat the oil in a small frying pan over a medium heat, add the onion and garlic and cook for 5 minutes. Add the bell pepper and tomato and cook for 3–4 minutes until soft.

Season with the thyme, black pepper and paprika. Carefully stir in the ackee and simmer for 5 minutes.

Fried plantain

2 ripe plantain, peeled and sliced
Vegetable oil, for shallow frying
Salt

Heat enough oil in a frying pan for shallow-frying over a medium heat. Cook the plantain slices for 1–2 minutes each side until golden brown. Remove from the oil, drain on kitchen paper and sprinkle with a likkle salt.

Cabbage

1 tsp olive oil
1 tbsp vegan butter
70g white cabbage, shredded

Heat the oil and butter in a small pan over a low heat, add the shredded cabbage and cook for 5–7 minutes.

Callaloo

1 tsp vegan butter
1 small onion, finely chopped
2 garlic cloves, finely chopped
¼ scotch bonnet pepper, deseeded and finely chopped
100g callaloo, or spinach
Salt and freshly ground black pepper

Melt the butter in a small pan over a medium heat. Add the onion, garlic and scotch bonnet and cook for 5 minutes until caramelised. Add the callaloo, season to taste with salt and black pepper and cook down for 5–7 minutes.

Spicy avocado, smashed plantain, bulgur wheat and peas, slaw, stew peas

A fusion of Caribbean- and South American-style cooking, this is a great, easy bowl, filled with raw and stripped back vegetables along with seasoned ones too. Somewhat an Ital version of a vegan Buddha bowl, this has a variation of flavours and textures, to provide the ultimate eating experience!

So simple to make, yet so delicious.

Spicy avocado

2 large avocados, peeled, stoned and diced
1 large tomato, diced
1 tsp salt
1 tsp freshly ground black pepper
1 tsp chilli flakes

Place the avocado in a mixing bowl with the tomato, salt, black pepper and chilli flakes, and mix to combine.

Smashed plantain

2 green plantain
Vegetable oil, for shallow-frying

Cut the top and bottom off the plantain, make a slit down the middle of the skin and peel. Cut into slices 2–3cm thick.

Heat the oil in a frying pan over a medium heat. Add the plantain slices and fry for 1–2 minutes each side until lightly golden. Remove to a board and use the base of a mug to crush them flat. Add back to the oil in the pan and fry again for a few minutes until crisp and golden brown.

Bulgur wheat and peas
See page 204

Slaw
See page 171

Stew peas
See page 44

Ital stew, boiled yam and plantain, callaloo

Ital stew is a popular dish in Jamaica because it can be eaten with almost anything! And this bowl of goodness is so delicious and quick and easy to make. The boiled yam soaks up the flava from the stew and the plantains and callaloo complement the dish so well. This is the kind of meal you can make on a low budget but it tastes like you're eating at a 5-star restaurant.

Ital stew
See page 123

Boiled yam and plantain

1 ripe plantain
125g white yam, peeled and cut into chunks

Bring a pan of salted water to the boil.
   Wash the plantain and pat dry, then cut off both ends and make a slit down the middle of the skin.
   Add the yam and plantain to the boiling water and cook over medium heat for 20 minutes until tender.
   Drain and peel the plantain, using tongs to hold it.

Callaloo
See page 65

Lentil and bean stew, callaloo fritters, curry tofu and vegetables, greens and beans, bulgur wheat and peas

People always ask how do you get protein from just eating vegetables? We say from this recipe right over yah-so. Lentils and beans contain lots of protein and are very filling. When you season di ting right it will bring you and everyone eating it joy! The bulgur wheat and peas are the perfect alternative to rice, and with the curry tofu and vegetables and greens and beans it will bring you a lighter but satisfying flava.

Lentil and bean stew
See page 115

Callaloo fritters
See page 48

Curry tofu and vegetables
See page 81

Greens and beans
See page 203

Bulgur wheat and peas
See page 204

Callaloo pesto pasta

Serves 6–8

A truly wonderful pasta dish that will bring a great experience to your taste buds – we added some spice to the traditional pesto flavours and it is so, so good! You can use any pasta, but we prefer spaghetti here as we love how the sauce drenches it so well. Callaloo is an earthy green vegetable that you can find fresh at your local veg market if you are near a Caribbean community, but you can also use spinach.
We're sure you'll enjoy this one!

Bring a large saucepan of salted water to the boil. Add the spaghetti and cook according to the packet instructions.

Meanwhile, in a separate large pan, heat 1 teaspoon of olive oil over a low heat, add the garlic and mustard seeds and fry for 5 minutes until caramelised.

Put the spinach, callaloo, scotch bonnet, basil, nuts, avocado, if using, ginger, lime juice, thyme and 2 tablespoons of olive oil into a blender or food processor. Add the fried garlic and mustard seeds. Just before the spaghetti is cooked, remove 150ml of the cooking water and add to the blender. Blend to a thick, creamy consistency and season to taste with salt and black pepper.

Back to the large pan: add 1 teaspoon of olive oil and the halved cherry tomatoes and cook down for 1–2 minutes, then add the blended pesto mixture and stir to combine and warm through.

Drain the spaghetti and add to the pan. Off the heat, toss to mix. Serve with grated Parmesan, extra nuts and a squeeze of lime juice.

500g dried spaghetti
Olive oil, for frying
4 garlic cloves, diced
1 tsp mustard seeds
300g spinach leaves, rinsed
1 x 340g can callaloo, well drained
1 scotch bonnet pepper, deseeded
15g basil (stalks and leaves)
75g walnuts or almonds, toasted, plus extra (optional), to serve
½ avocado (optional)
3cm piece of fresh ginger, peeled and roughly chopped
Juice of 1 lime, plus extra to serve
1 tsp dried thyme
300g cherry tomatoes, halved
50g vegan Parmesan-style cheese, grated
Salt and freshly ground black pepper

Rasta pumpkin pasta

Serves 6–8

A creamy plant-based thriller! Taking inspiration from traditional Rasta pasta which uses cheeses, we've created a vegan alternative with our creamy pumpkin sauce. Roasting the pumpkin with garlic and chilli helps give the sauce a zingy jump, before it's thickened in the pan to the creamiest sauce you'll see! Give this one a go – it's super-quick, easy and delicious!

Preheat the oven to 170°C Fan/190°C/Gas 5.

Place a sheet of baking parchment on a baking tray. Add the diced pumpkin or squash, garlic bulb and scotch bonnet or chilli, then sprinkle 2 tablespoons of olive oil and 1 teaspoon each of salt and black pepper pon it and mix together. Roast in the oven for 25 minutes until cooked through and starting to caramelise.

Leave to cool for 5 minutes, then dash into a blender, squeezing the soft garlic cloves out of their papery skins. Add the yoghurt, rosemary and thyme and crumble in the stock cube. Add half the coconut milk, the syrup, salt to taste and a splash of water. Blend together until smooth.

Bring a large saucepan of salted water to the boil. Add the pasta and cook according to the packet instructions, then drain.

Meanwhile, in a large saucepan, heat 2 tablespoons of olive oil until hot. Add the onion and bell peppers and sauté for 5 minutes until soft, then add in the blended pumpkin sauce, remaining coconut milk and jerk paste. Stir, then simmer, uncovered, for 5 minutes until thickened.

Add the drained pasta to the sauce and combine well to coat. Add a sprinkling of parsley and enjoy.

- 500g pumpkin or butternut squash, peeled, deseeded and diced
- 1 whole garlic bulb
- 1 scotch bonnet or chilli pepper, deseeded and chopped
- Olive oil, for cooking
- 200g coconut yoghurt
- Leaves of 2 rosemary sprigs
- 6 fresh thyme sprigs or 1½ tsp dried thyme
- 1 vegan stock cube
- 1 x 400ml can coconut milk
- 1 tbsp golden syrup
- 500g dried penne pasta
- 1 onion, sliced
- 1 red bell pepper, deseeded and sliced
- 1 green bell pepper, deseeded and sliced
- 1 yellow bell pepper, deseeded and sliced
- 1 tbsp jerk paste
- Salt and freshly ground black pepper
- Handful of parsley, chopped, to serve

Spicy bolognese

This is one of our go-to midweek flava favourites, and all done in under 30 minutes! Growing up, bolognese was a boring dinner (sorry Mum!), but as we got older we began to actually love and miss it. This vegan-mince version, using Caribbean spices and seasonings, is just so, so good! It never lets us down and won't let you down either.

We serve it here with spaghetti, but why not have a cheeky garlic hard-dough bread (see page 198) with it too!

Heat the coconut oil and butter in a large pan, add the onion, garlic, spring onions and carrot and cook down for 5–7 minutes until soft. Fling in the mushrooms and cook for a further 3 minutes.

Add the mince and cook, stirring, for 5–7 minutes until browned all over, then add the tomato purée and stock, stir and season with salt, the thyme, black pepper and pimento. Add the scotch bonnet and cook for a further 7–8 minutes.

Meanwhile, bring a large saucepan of salted water to the boil. Add the spaghetti and cook according to the packet instructions, then drain.

Remove the scotch bonnet from the bolognese and serve over the spaghetti, with grated Parmesan on top.

2 tbsp coconut oil
1 tbsp vegan butter
1 small onion, finely chopped
2 garlic cloves, finely chopped
2 spring onions, thinly sliced
1 carrot, finely diced
200g chestnut mushrooms, finely chopped
300g meat-free mince
5 tbsp tomato purée
200ml vegan stock
1 tbsp dried thyme
1 tsp freshly ground black pepper
1 tsp ground pimento (allspice)
1 scotch bonnet pepper
350g dried spaghetti
Salt
Grated vegan Parmesan-style cheese, to serve

Tomato and coconut pasta

Serves 4–6

Craig is a massive Italian food fan. He met a lovely Italian family while on holiday in Jamaica a while back, which had a big influence on this recipe – fusing Caribbean flavas with Italian dishes. Blending the tomatoes, coconut and spices really allows them to infuse with the pasta. The addition of vegan cheese provides the extra creaminess.

Bring a large saucepan of salted water to the boil. Add the pasta and cook according to the packet instructions, taking a few minutes off the suggested cooking time (it will cook further in the sauce).

Meanwhile, put the tomatoes, garlic, coconut milk, coconut cream, spring onions and scotch bonnet in a blender and blend until smooth. Season with salt and black pepper to taste, and add a drizzle of olive oil.

Add the mixture to a frying pan, place over a medium-high heat, bring to a bubble and cook for 5–7 minutes, then add the parsley and cherry tomatoes and cook down for about 5 minutes until the tomatoes are soft. Add the thyme, all-purpose seasoning and cheese, and give it a mix.

When the pasta is nearly cooked, drain, add to the frying pan and mix di ting together. Simmer for 5 minutes until thick before serving with the toasted coconut sprinkled over, if you like.

300g dried rigatoni pasta
4–6 large ripe tomatoes or
   1 x 400g can tomatoes
4 garlic cloves, peeled
1 x 400ml can coconut milk
200g coconut cream
3 spring onions, sliced
¼ scotch bonnet pepper, deseeded
Drizzle of olive oil
10g parsley leaves, chopped
6–8 cherry tomatoes, halved
1 tbsp dried thyme
1½ tsp all-purpose seasoning
75g vegan cheese, grated
Salt and freshly ground black pepper
40g desiccated coconut, toasted,
   to garnish (optional)

Sweet and sour tofu

Chinese takeaway is something that, as a family, we used to always enjoy on a Friday night, as it was a break from cooking. Tofu is an ingredient that's eaten in Jamaica a lot so this sweet and sour tofu recipe is the perfect fakeaway to enjoy at the weekend. The tofu is crispy on the outside and tender on the inside, with a sweet, spicy sauce that completes this comforting meal. Serve with steamed rice and garnish with spring onions if you like. Delicious!

First make the sweet and sour sauce. Heat the vegetable oil in a small saucepan over a low-medium heat. Add the remaining ingredients, stir, bring to the boil then turn down the heat and simmer for 10 minutes. Remove from the heat and set aside.

Drain off any water in the packet of tofu, place a plate on top of the block and press down on it for 30 seconds, then blot with kitchen paper to remove as much water as you can. Cut into cubes and add to a bowl. Add the cornflour, Chinese five-spice and salt and black pepper to taste, then toss the tofu cubes to fully coat them.

Heat the olive oil in a non-stick frying pan or wok, and carefully add the tofu pieces to the hot oil. Pan-fry for a few minutes on each side until golden brown. Tip out into a bowl and set aside. Heat the sesame oil in the same pan over a high heat, add the garlic and ginger and caramelise for 5 minutes, then add the spring onions, red onion, broccoli and bell peppers and cook down until softening. Add the fried tofu back to the pan, then stir in the sweet and sour sauce. Simmer for 5 minutes, before serving with rice.

1 x 420g block of firm tofu
3 tbsp cornflour
1 tbsp Chinese five-spice
1 tbsp olive oil
2 tbsp sesame oil
4–6 garlic cloves, very finely chopped
1 tbsp very finely chopped fresh ginger
2 spring onions, sliced
1 small red onion, chopped
100g broccoli florets
2 bell peppers, ideally different colours, deseeded and cut into 3–4cm chunks
Salt and freshly ground black pepper

For the sweet and sour sauce

3 tbsp vegetable oil
4–6 garlic cloves, finely chopped
1 tbsp chilli flakes
250ml water
2 tbsp tomato ketchup
1 tbsp hot sauce
2 tbsp dark soy sauce
1 tbsp rice vinegar or white vinegar
2 tbsp maple syrup
150g fresh pineapple, diced

Curry tofu and vegetables

Serves 4

A light, quick and easy one-pot to make at home. Tofu is used quite often in Jamaica by the Rastafarian community, and curried is one of the ways they cook it down. We've flung our own flava at it, and it's one of our favourite munches. Juicy flavours, crunch, taste...

First, prepare your tofu. After draining off any water in the packet, place a plate on top of the block of tofu and press down on it for 30 seconds, then blot with kitchen paper to remove as much water as you can. Cut into chunky cubes, about 2–3cm, place in a bowl and add the all-purpose seasoning, curry powder, ginger and olive oil. Cover and set aside to marinate.

Heat 4 tablespoons of the oil in a large frying pan or wok over a medium heat. Add the onions, spring onions, cabbage, carrot and bell peppers and cook down for 5–7 minutes until softened, then add the garlic and ginger and stir well. Remove everything from the pan and set aside.

Add the remaining 1 tablespoon of oil to the pan and heat. Add the marinated tofu and fry for a few minutes on each side until golden brown. Add the coconut milk and water and stir well. In a small bowl, mix together the cornflour and curry powder, add a likkle water to make a smooth paste, then add to the pan. Mix together and simmer for 5–7 minutes, to thicken. Stir the veggies back in and simmer for 5 minutes to heat through.

5 tbsp olive oil
½ red onion, thinly sliced
½ white onion, thinly sliced
2 spring onions, thinly sliced
¼ white cabbage, shredded
1 carrot, cut into julienne
½ green bell pepper, deseeded and cut into julienne
½ red bell pepper, deseeded and cut into julienne
2 garlic cloves, finely chopped
1 tbsp grated fresh ginger
1 x 400ml can coconut milk or coconut cream
125ml water
1 tsp cornflour
1 tbsp Caribbean curry powder

For the tofu
1 x 200g block of extra-firm tofu
1 tbsp all-purpose seasoning
1 tbsp Caribbean curry powder
1 tsp grated fresh ginger
1 tbsp olive oil

Spicy coconut ramen

Serves 4

We've taken a Japanese ramen recipe and given it a Caribbean twist. We absolutely love ramen – it's one of our favourites to have if we want to switch it up a bit for lunch or dinner.

And this recipe is oh so lovely – it has a garlic-coconut-infused broth, cradling some meaty mushrooms and spicy flavours. It's a super-easy recipe as well. We normally use ramen noodles, but like to switch it up sometimes by using udon, egg noodles or rice noodles – feel free to do the same, whatever your preference.

In a small bowl, make the miso glaze by combining all the ingredients, then set aside.

For the tofu, drain off any water in the packet, then place a plate on top of the block of tofu and press down on it for 30 seconds, then blot with kitchen paper to remove as much water as you can. Cut the tofu into 4 slices about 1–2cm thick.

Heat the olive oil in a frying pan. Dip the tofu slices in the miso glaze, add to the hot oil and fry for 3–4 minutes on each side. Remove and set aside. Add a likkle more oil to the pan, add the pak choi, mushrooms and garlic and cook down for about 3–4 minutes until soft. Set aside.

Heat the stock and coconut milk together gently in a large pan. Add the scotch bonnet and simmer for 10 minutes. Add your noodles and cook for a few minutes, according to the packet instructions.

Meanwhile, in a mixing bowl, combine the tahini, rice vinegar, soy sauce, sesame oil and chilli oil, then whisk into the hot broth. Ladle the broth into individual bowls, removing the scotch bonnet and dividing the noodles evenly between each. Add the mushrooms and pak choi and top with the slices of fried tofu and spring onions to finish.

1 x 200g block of firm tofu
4 tbsp olive oil, plus extra for the veg
2 pak choi, quartered lengthways
150g oyster mushrooms (or any of your choice)
2 garlic cloves, finely chopped
500ml vegan stock
150ml coconut milk
1 scotch bonnet pepper
300g ramen or flat rice noodles (or any of your choice)
1 tbsp tahini
1 tbsp rice vinegar
1 tbsp dark soy sauce
1 tbsp sesame oil
1 tbsp chilli oil
2 spring onions, thinly sliced, to finish

For the miso glaze

2 tsp miso
1 tbsp golden syrup
1 tsp browning or 1 tbsp dark soy sauce
1 tbsp sesame oil

Mushroom pepper steak

Serves 4–6

This is the plant-based version of Jamaican pepper steak. Mushroom has that meaty texture that gives you the perfect substitute, so we have re-created the iconic dish to make a lighter, plant-based version that even meat eaters will love. The juicy texture of mushrooms soaks up flavas so well. Serve with bulgur wheat and peas (see page 204), fried plantain (see page 65) and slaw (see page 171).

Add the mushrooms to a mixing bowl and season with salt and black pepper to taste. Add the all-purpose seasoning, thyme sprigs and browning and mix together to coat the mushrooms.

Heat half the oil in a frying pan over a medium heat, add the mushrooms and cook for 5 minutes, stirring occasionally, until browned and all the liquid released during cooking has evaporated, then tip into a bowl.

Add the remaining oil to the pan, add the onion, garlic, bell peppers and spring onions and cook for 5 minutes until starting to caramelise. Add the stock granules with ¼ teaspoon of browning and the water, and stir together. Add the mushrooms back to the pan and simmer for 5 minutes. Serve with bulgur wheat and peas, fried plantain and slaw.

300g Portobello mushrooms, sliced
1 tsp all-purpose seasoning
4–6 fresh thyme sprigs
½ tsp browning or 1½ tsp dark soy sauce, plus a little extra to finish
2 tbsp olive oil
1 medium onion, sliced
4 garlic cloves, very finely chopped
3 bell peppers (1 green, 1 red and 1 yellow), deseeded and cut into thin strips
2 spring onions, sliced
2 tbsp vegan stock granules
240ml water
Salt and freshly ground black pepper

Baked sweet potatoes with spicy chickpea mayo

Serves 4

You can't go wrong with a baked potato – affordable and versatile, and you won't ever be disappointed by it! Growing up, it was a common thing to see tuna on jacket potatoes at school, but we've transformed it by replacing the tuna with chickpeas and using sweet potatoes for added flava and colour.

Preheat the oven to 180°C Fan/200°C/Gas 6.

Place the sweet potatoes on a baking tray and bake in the oven for 30–40 minutes until soft all the way through.

Meanwhile, add the chickpeas, onion, mayo, lemon juice, garlic powder, thyme, chilli flakes and parsley to a bowl, and use a fork to crush the chickpeas and mix everything together.

Cut the sweet potatoes down the middle and squeeze lightly to open them up. Spoon the chickpea mixture into the middle, sprinkle over some parsley, spoon over some scotch bonnet sauce and serve.

4 sweet potatoes, washed and dried
2 x 400g cans chickpeas, drained and rinsed
1 red onion, finely diced
4 tbsp vegan mayo
Squeeze of lemon juice
1 tsp garlic powder
1 tsp dried thyme
2 tsp chilli flakes
2 tbsp chopped fresh parsley, plus extra to serve
Scotch bonnet sauce (see page 215), to serve

Aubergines stuffed with spicy gungo peas

Serves 4

Gungo peas, also known as pigeon peas, are very popular in the Caribbean community, and often used as the peas in rice and peas, but if you can't find them, canned kidney beans will work just as well. To give this fun and simple dish a more universal flavour, we have added some olives and baked it with cheese on top.

Now it's all about tucking in and enjoying the food...

Preheat the oven to 180°C Fan/200°C/Gas 6.

Cut each aubergine in half lengthways. Using a spoon, scoop out the flesh from each, leaving a 2.5cm thick layer around the sides and on the base; reserve the flesh. Place the aubergine shells on a baking tray, drizzle over 2 tablespoons of the oil and bake in the oven for 30 minutes until softened but not collapsed.

Meanwhile, heat the remaining oil in a pan, add the onion, garlic and scotch bonnet and cook down for 5–7 minutes until soft. Add the all-purpose seasoning, tomato purée, tomatoes, bell pepper, gungo peas and the reserved aubergine flesh and cook down, stirring occasionally, until softened. Stir in the parsley and olives and simmer for 5 minutes.

Spoon the mixture into the baked aubergine halves, sprinkle over the mozzarella and place back in the oven for 20 minutes until the cheese is melted and bubbling. Serve garnished with parsley.

2 large aubergines
3 tbsp olive oil
1 medium red onion, finely chopped
2 garlic cloves, finely chopped
½ scotch bonnet pepper, deseeded and diced
1 tbsp all-purpose seasoning
1 tbsp tomato purée
2 large tomatoes, diced
1 green bell pepper, deseeded and diced
1 x 400g can gungo peas, drained and rinsed
Handful of fresh parsley leaves, chopped, plus extra to garnish
Handful of black olives, pitted
100g grated vegan mozzarella-style cheese

Cauliflower burger with spicy mayo, slaw and mango chutney

Serves 4

This one is just mind-blowing: indescribable flavas that leave you lost for words! For those who are new to this vegan life, and don't get too excited when you think about cauliflower in a burger... we were the same at first, but trust us, this tastes just like a chicken burger!! Fried this way, you'll be thinking, 'cauliflower, where have you been all my life?!' Such a wow burger, and we've added a slaw topping and mango chutney to put the perfect touch to it.

YOU. WILL. LOVE. IT!

First wash your cauliflower, then slice into 4 thick, steak-sized pieces. Bring a large saucepan of water to the boil, add the cauliflower and boil for 5 minutes. Drain and transfer to a tray lined with kitchen paper to cool a likkle.

Make the sauce by combining the mayo, hot pepper sauce and parsley in a small bowl. To make the slaw, combine the cabbage, carrot, scotch bonnet, vinegar, mango chutney and salt in a separate bowl.

Get two large, deep bowls. Pour the coconut milk into one and stir in the all-purpose seasoning, salt and black pepper. In the second bowl combine the flour, cornflour, curry powder, paprika, garlic powder and thyme. Coat the cauliflower first in the coconut milk, then the dry ingredients, and repeat (to give an extra-crunchy layer).

Heat enough oil for shallow-frying in a large frying pan over a high heat. Add the cauliflower (you might need to do this in two batches), turn the heat down to medium-high and fry for about 3 minutes on each side until golden brown. Remove to a tray lined with kitchen paper, to drain.

Build the burger on the base of a toasted burger bun, adding a spoonful of sauce, then a cauliflower steak and a layer of spicy slaw. Spoon over some mango chutney and add the top of the bun.

Now it's time to nyam!

1 large head of cauliflower (about 600g)
200ml coconut milk (or any plant-based milk)
2 tbsp all-purpose seasoning
1 tsp salt
1 tsp freshly ground black pepper
250g plain flour
1 tsp cornflour
1 tbsp curry powder
1 tsp paprika
1 tsp garlic powder
1 tsp dried thyme
Vegetable oil, for shallow-frying
4 vegan brioche burger buns, toasted

For the sauce
4 tbsp vegan mayo
2 tsp hot pepper sauce
Small handful of parsley, finely chopped

For the slaw
¼ white cabbage, shredded
1 carrot, grated
¼ scotch bonnet pepper, deseeded and thinly sliced
1 tsp apple cider vinegar
1 tbsp mango chutney, plus extra to serve
Pinch of salt

Caribbean bangers and mash

Serves 2

Bangers and mash, a traditional dish of Britain, so iconic and popular we wanted to recreate it in a vegan way and with more Caribbean style, adding more FLAVA! Vegan sausages in a saucy stew, served with soft creamy plantain mash... the best combination ever.

Preheat the oven to 180ºC Fan/200ºC/Gas 6.

Firstly, season your sausages with the jerk paste and all-purpose seasoning, coating them all over. Place on an oven tray and dash in the oven for 10 minutes.

Meanwhile, for the plantain mash, cook the plantain in a pan of boiling water for 10 minutes until tender, then drain, return to the pan and add the milk and butter, with salt and black pepper to taste. Mash well with a potato masher.

While the plantain is boiling, heat the oil in a medium frying pan over a high heat, add the onion and garlic and fry for a few minutes until caramelised. Mix in the browning, stock granules, water and cornflour paste to combine, then add the browned sausages and cook for 5 minutes until cooked through. Garnish with the scotch bonnet and parsley and serve with the plantain mash, and a green veg such as peas.

6 vegan sausages
2 tbsp jerk paste
½ tbsp all-purpose seasoning
2 tbsp olive oil
1 small red onion, sliced into rings
2 garlic cloves, chopped
1 tsp browning or 1 tbsp dark
    soy sauce
1 tbsp vegan stock granules
240ml water
1 tsp cornflour mixed to a paste
    with a likkle water
¼ scotch bonnet pepper, finely
    chopped
1 tbsp chopped fresh parsley

For the plantain mash
2 ripe plantain, peeled and chopped
100ml soy milk
1 tbsp vegan butter
Salt and freshly ground black pepper

Veggie dumpling pizza

Makes 2

Using a Jamaican fried dumpling base and juicy veggies pon top, OMG this is just incredibly flavalicious! How did we not think of this sooner in life?!

Growing up, eating fried dumpling was something we looked forward to – its crunchy exterior and soft buttery inside is something of heaven. And we've cooked down a blend of our favourite Caribbean and everyday veggies as the topping with vegan cheese. Now we just can't go back to the standard pizza bases. Give this one a go – friends, family, kids will love it.

For the dumpling base, add the flour to a mixing bowl along with the melted butter or oil, salt and water, then mix together and knead into a smooth ball. Wrap in cling film and put in the fridge to rest for 30 minutes.

Meanwhile, put a likkle vegetable oil into a frying pan over a high heat, add the onion, garlic and scotch bonnet and cook for 10 minutes until softened. Add the bell peppers, broccoli, courgette, cherry tomatoes, okra, ginger and herb sprigs. Add the pimento and some salt and black pepper to taste, mix together, then cover and cook down over a medium heat for 3–5 minutes until softened.

Preheat the oven to 180°C Fan/200°C/Gas 6.

Take your dumpling dough from the fridge and dust your work surface and hands with flour. Cut the dough in half, shape each half into a ball then roll out into round pizza bases, about 22cm in diameter.

Heat enough oil in a large frying pan for shallow-frying, add the pizza bases one at a time and fry for 3–4 minutes on each side until golden brown. Place the bases on an oven tray and spread with the tomato purée, then cover with the grated cheese and the veggie mix. Sprinkle on the sweetcorn and bake in the oven for 12–15 minutes until the top is golden, then serve.

Vegetable oil, for cooking
1 red onion, diced
2 garlic cloves, crushed
1 scotch bonnet pepper, deseeded and diced
½ red bell pepper, deseeded and chopped
½ yellow bell pepper, deseeded and chopped
6–8 broccoli florets, halved
½ courgette, sliced
6–8 cherry tomatoes, halved
4 okra, halved widthways
1 tbsp grated fresh ginger
3–4 fresh herbs sprigs of your choice
1 tsp ground pimento (allspice)
80–100g tomato purée
120g vegan cheese, grated
25g frozen or canned sweetcorn
Salt and freshly ground black pepper

For the dumpling base
400g self-raising flour, plus extra for dusting
1 tbsp melted vegan butter or oil
½ tsp salt
250ml water

S &
STEWS

Curries and Stews

Bwoiii the Caribbean is surely home to some of the best curries and stews ina di world! So warm, thick and full of so many flavour combinations and spices it's unreal.

We've eaten our fair share of these in our time, and can honestly say it's very hard to find one as good as a vegetable version: the variety of textures, the wholesome taste, and the unique Caribbean method make it such an enjoyable dish.

Heavily influenced by the Ital diet, Caribbean curries are iconic for their pairing of multiple flavours and earthy vegetables like green banana, pumpkin and plantain, and spices that hit you in the right spots – cumin, lemongrass and allspice. These deep-flavoured dishes are really easy to cook and you're guaranteed to love them. We've got your Saturday curry night and midweek speedy curries sorted, packed full of nuff flava and authenticity.

Cooking methods and flavours from countries like Trinidad and Tobago and Guyana are heavily influential in this chapter. Buckle your seat belts, as you're about to take a trip to a tropical location: your kitchen!

Curries and Stews

Caribbean green seasoning curry   Serves 4–6

We love a Thai green curry, so we've taken inspiration from it and fused it with the flavours of Caribbean green seasoning – a seasoning mix often used in Trinidadian curries as a base for cooking chunky vegetables, and oh my, the flavas are incredible!

First, we're going to blend up the Caribbean green seasoning. Trim and roughly chop any ingredients that need breaking down a little, then add to a blender with salt and black pepper to taste, and blitz to a thick but still sloppy consistency. Add a likkle water if it needs it.

Heat the vegetable oil in a large pan, add the bell pepper, aubergine and green beans and fry for 5–7 minutes, then remove from the pan.

Add 4 tablespoons of the green seasoning mixture to the pan (save the rest in the fridge, where it will keep in a sealed jar for a week). Cook down for 2–3 minutes, then add the cumin, curry powder and paprika and mix together. Add the coconut milk, soy sauce, sugar and stock and bring to the boil. Reduce the heat and simmer for 5 minutes.

Add in the pan-fried vegetables and mix it all together, then squeeze over the lime juice and serve with plain rice, with coriander leaves sprinkled on top.

2 tbsp vegetable oil
1 red bell pepper, deseeded and cut into strips
1 large aubergine, cut into half-moon slices about 1cm thick
250g green beans
1 tsp ground cumin
1 tsp Caribbean curry powder
1 tsp paprika
200ml coconut milk
1 tbsp dark soy sauce
2 tbsp brown sugar
350ml vegan stock
Juice of 2 limes
Small handful of coriander leaves, to serve

For the green seasoning
Handful of coriander leaves
Handful of parsley leaves
4 garlic cloves, peeled
2 spring onions
1 celery stick
½ medium onion
3cm piece of fresh ginger
1 lemongrass stalk
4 fresh thyme sprigs
½ scotch bonnet pepper
200ml coconut milk
Salt and freshly ground black pepper

Green banana curry

Serves 4–6

A thick and hearty curry that will leave ya belly full! The green banana, which is the unripe version of a banana, is a starchy Caribbean staple vegetable. It is used often in soups and stews, and here in this curry because it's such a fantastic absorber and contributor to the sauce. It brings a rich thickness to the curry that honestly no other vegetable can bring. And the flava too – wow! You'll absolutely love it!

Cut both ends off each green banana, score a line down the middle of the skin from top to bottom, then cut each in half across the middle (to give you two shorter lengths).

Bring a large saucepan of water to the boil, add the green bananas and cook for 20 minutes until soft. Drain and carefully peel off the skin, using tongs to hold the banana, then set aside to cool down a likkle.

Heat the coconut oil in a large pan over a medium heat, add the onion, scotch bonnet, garlic, ginger and curry powder and cook down for 5–7 minutes until soft. Add the coconut milk and tomatoes, carrots, pumpkin or squash, chickpeas, bell peppers and green bananas, and mix together. Add the pimento and thyme, season with salt and black pepper to taste, then simmer for 10 minutes.

When the veg is done, throw in the spinach and syrup, check for seasoning and allow the spinach to wilt before serving with brown rice.

3 green (unripe) bananas
2 tbsp coconut oil
1 onion, diced
1 scotch bonnet pepper, deseeded and diced
4 garlic cloves, chopped
1 tbsp grated fresh ginger
2 tbsp Caribbean curry powder
1 x 400ml can coconut milk
4 tomatoes, diced
2 carrots, thickly sliced
500g pumpkin or butternut squash, deseeded and cut into wedges
1 x 400g can chickpeas, drained and rinsed
1 green bell pepper, deseeded and cut into strips
1 orange bell pepper, deseeded and cut into strips
¼ tsp ground pimento (allspice)
¼ tsp dried thyme
Handful of spinach leaves
1 tbsp golden syrup
Salt and freshly ground black pepper

Curries and Stews

Curry jackfruit

This is a really simple and quick, hearty curry dish, using traditional Caribbean flavours, with a rich coconut kick. We marinate jackfruit chunks in the same way we'd marinate meat, then cook it down in coconut milk with potatoes.

Like all curries we have to nyam this pon some white rice. It's a must!

Add the jackfruit to a mixing bowl with the curry powder, ginger, salt, black pepper, onion, garlic, thyme and pimento. Mix together and leave to marinate for 10 minutes.

In a large frying pan, heat the coconut oil over a medium heat, add the marinated jackfruit mixture and cook for 5 minutes, to caramelise and add some colour, then add the coconut milk, water and potato. Stir together and cook for 20 minutes until the potato is tender. Serve with rice and steamed cabbage.

1 x 560g can young green jackfruit in brine, drained and rinsed
3 tbsp Caribbean curry powder
1 tsp grated fresh ginger
1 tsp salt
1 tsp freshly ground black pepper
1 small onion, finely chopped
4 garlic cloves, chopped
4–6 fresh thyme sprigs
1 tsp ground pimento (allspice)
2 tbsp coconut oil
1 x 400ml can coconut milk
250ml water
1 large potato, peeled cut into 3cm cubes

Coconut, black-eyed pea and sweet potato curry

Serves 4–6

Beans (aka peas) are popular in the Caribbean; they are a great source of protein and bring a delicious depth to curries! This dish has a flava-filled and uniquely spiced curry base, with cinnamon and mustard seeds bringing a wonderful aroma.

Serve with white rice and a splash of coconut milk for a dinner to savour with NUFF FLAVA!

Heat the oil in a large saucepan over a medium heat, add the mustard seeds and toast for 1 minute, then add the onion, garlic, cinnamon stick and bay leaves and cook for about 5 minutes until the onion softens. Add the turmeric, curry powder, thyme and ginger. Stir over a low heat for 2–3 minutes, to allow the spices to infuse.

Add the sweet potatoes, scotch bonnet or chilli flakes and tomatoes and cook, stirring, for 5 minutes until the tomatoes soften. Add the black-eyed peas and the water, then add the coconut milk, holding back a few tablespoons. Fling in some salt and black pepper to taste, increase to a simmer and cook for 7 minutes.

Garnish with coriander and the reserved coconut milk, and serve with lime wedges and rice.

2 tbsp vegetable oil
1 tsp mustard seeds
1 medium onion, diced
3 garlic cloves, diced
1 cinnamon stick
2 bay leaves
1 tsp ground turmeric
2 tbsp Caribbean curry powder
Bunch of fresh thyme
1 thumb-sized piece
   of fresh ginger, grated
2 sweet potatoes, peeled and
   chopped in chunks
½ scotch bonnet pepper, deseeded
   and diced, or 2 tsp chilli flakes
2 tomatoes, chopped
2 x 400g cans black-eyed peas,
   drained and rinsed
250ml water
1 x 400ml can coconut milk
Salt and freshly ground black pepper

To serve
Coriander leaves
Lime wedges

Sweet potato and chickpea peanut stew with jollof rice

Serves 4

We've always had a strong core of African friends, so have been exposed to the vibrant and wonderful flavours of jollof rice quite a lot. Shaun's fiancée is Ghanaian, so we've always swung towards their native version, and we love it so much!

Often eaten with a dry meat, we've created this nutty sweet potato and chickpea stew to go alongside it instead; it just blends so well together and the rich depth of flavours is something you'll love.

Add some fried plantain and make it a real African treat for dinner!

First, make the jollof rice. Place one onion half with the bell pepper, garlic, scotch bonnet, tomatoes (roughly chopped if using fresh), water and salt to taste in a blender, and blitz until combined. Dice the remaining onion half.

In a medium saucepan, heat the coconut oil over a high heat, add the diced onion and tomato purée and cook for 5 minutes. Add the blended mixture to the pan, stir and bring to the boil. Season with salt and the all-purpose seasoning then add the rice, cover and cook over a low heat for 25 minutes until the rice is cooked, stirring it halfway through. Remove from the heat and keep covered until ready to serve.

Meanwhile, for the stew, heat the coconut oil in a large saucepan over a medium heat, add the red onion, tomato purée and ginger and cook for 5 minutes, then add the peanut butter, all-purpose seasoning and stock. Mix together and season with salt and pepper to taste. Add the sweet potato and cook for 20 minutes until tender and the sauce is reduced, then add the chickpeas and kale and simmer for a further 5 minutes.

Plate up with the jollof rice, and some fried plantain if you like.

For the jollof rice
1 red onion, halved
1 red bell pepper, deseeded and roughly chopped
2 garlic cloves, peeled
1 scotch bonnet pepper, deseeded
2 large tomatoes or 1 x 400g can tomatoes
100ml water
1 tbsp coconut oil
2 tbsp tomato purée
1 tbsp all-purpose seasoning
200g long-grain rice, rinsed

For the stew
1 tbsp coconut oil
1 small red onion, diced
2 tbsp tomato purée
1 tsp grated fresh ginger
3 tbsp peanut butter
1 tbsp all-purpose seasoning
750ml vegan stock
1 large sweet potato, peeled and cubed
1 x 400g can chickpeas, drained and rinsed
100g kale, chopped
Salt and freshly ground black pepper

Curried chickpea plantain boat   Serves 2

Wow wow wow, you've got to give this recipe a try. Stop flicking through the pages, thinking, 'What am I gone make today?'. This is your answer! You cannot go wrong. Nuff flava in ah dis! We love this recipe, it's a feel-good one. Oven-baked plantain, so soft and melt-in-the-mouth with a creamy, crunchy, coconut-spiced chickpea curry pon top! It's a truly fantastic meal that you will absolutely love!

Plantains really do make this recipe, but you can use sweet potatoes instead. That tastes pretty amazing too.

Preheat the oven to 180°C Fan/200°C/Gas 6.

Score a line down the middle of each peeled plantain, stopping just before you reach each end and carefully ease the two halves apart slightly. Add to a mixing bowl with the salt, black pepper, paprika and thyme or mixed herbs. Drizzle with olive oil and mix together, making sure the plantain is well covered with the seasonings. Transfer to a roasting dish and roast in the oven for 40 minutes until cooked through.

Meanwhile, in a frying pan, heat the coconut oil over a medium heat, add the onion and garlic and cook down for 5–7 minutes until soft, then add the curry powder and grated ginger and cook down until golden brown. Add the coconut milk and bring to the boil, then add the chickpeas and all-purpose seasoning and a likkle more curry powder, and cook for 5–7 minutes until thickened.

Take the plantain out of the oven, transfer to plates and open up the middle of each. Spoon over the chickpea curry then garnish with parsley and scotch bonnet to serve.

4 ripe plantain, peeled
1 tsp salt
1 tsp freshly ground black pepper
1 tbsp paprika
1 tsp dried thyme or mixed herbs
Olive oil, to drizzle
2 tbsp coconut oil
1 small onion, diced
2 garlic cloves, finely chopped
4 tsp Caribbean curry powder, plus a likkle extra
1 tsp grated fresh ginger
1 x 400ml can coconut milk
300g canned chickpeas, rinsed
1 tbsp all-purpose seasoning
Parsley leaves and some finely diced scotch bonnet pepper, to garnish

Curries and Stews   111

Curry butter beans

Serves 4–6

A real stress-free, super-easy, vegan flava for you guys! With most of the ingredients from your store cupboard or fridge, it's a perfect midweek comfort dinner.

We had butter beans quite a lot growing up, in meat-based dishes like oxtail; they soak up curry and stew flavours so well. And often we looked forward to eating them more than meat! So we really enjoy this dish, and we're sure you and your loved ones will too.

Canned butter beans usually don't take too long to cook down, but we really like these as tender as possible, so don't rush the simmering process.

Heat the oil in a large pan, dash in the onion, bell pepper, carrot and garlic, and cook down for 5–7 minutes until soft. Add the curry powder, thyme, ginger, chilli flakes, salt and black pepper to taste, plus a likkle splash of water, and stir to create a thick curry paste.

Add in the butter beans and mix it all together. Fill up the empty bean cans with water and fling into the pan, along with the paprika. Mix together and simmer for 15–20 minutes until the butter beans are really tender, topping up with a likkle more water if needed.

Serve with white rice, fried plantain and avocado salad. You'll love it!

1 tbsp vegetable oil
1 onion, finely chopped
1 green or red bell pepper, deseeded and finely chopped
1 medium carrot, finely chopped
2 garlic cloves, chopped
2½ tbsp Caribbean curry powder
1 tsp dried thyme
1 tsp ground ginger
1 tsp chilli flakes
2 x 400g cans butter beans, drained and rinsed
1 tsp paprika
Salt and freshly ground black pepper

Lentil and bean stew

Serves 4

This is a comforting stew packed full of protein. If you're looking for something filling and healthy for the whole family to enjoy, this is your go-to recipe. A versatile dish where you can use any vegetables you have in your fridge. Best eaten with a likkle rice, or it's even great on its own. Any leftovers are delicious in one of our flava bowls on pages 64–67.

Heat the oil in a saucepan over a medium heat, then dash in your red onion and garlic. Cook for 5–7 minutes until golden.

Add the carrots, spring onions and celery, stir and continue to cook down for 5 minutes. Add the tomatoes and cook for 5 minutes, stirring occasionally, to create a saucy stew. Stir in the beans and lentils, add the chilli powder and season with salt and black pepper to taste. Cook for 15 minutes, then add the thyme and scotch bonnet and simmer for a final 5 minutes. Remove the scotch bonnet before serving.

4 tbsp olive oil
1 red onion, diced
2 garlic cloves, diced
2 carrots, diced
2 spring onions, sliced
2 celery sticks, diced
1 x 400g can chopped tomatoes
1 x 400g can Caribbean mixed beans (peas and beans), drained and rinsed
1 x 400g can green lentils, drained
1 tsp chilli powder
3 fresh thyme sprigs
1 scotch bonnet pepper
Salt and freshly ground black pepper

Creamy mushroom and okra stew

Serves 4

Mushrooms have to be one of our fave ingredients to use; they have a similar texture to meat, but with all that plant-based goodness in them, and we love this dish – our go-to quick and hearty dinner.

The stew is rich in flava, and is so filling, too. Okra is a proper sick addition to this one; the texture is unique, but you want to make sure you don't cook it too long or it will be slimy – just a likkle simmer towards the end so the crunch will still be there.

Served alongside fried plantain, quinoa and kale or spinach, it's a beautiful bowl of FLAVAFUL DELICIOUSNESS.

Heat the coconut oil in a large frying pan over a medium heat, add the onion, garlic, carrot and potato and stir for a couple of minutes. Add the mushrooms and cook down for a few minutes, then add the coconut milk, black pepper and pimento and cook down for 10 minutes until creamy.

Add the basil, thyme and okra and simmer for 5 minutes. Season to taste with salt and serve.

2 tbsp coconut oil
1 onion, diced
4 garlic cloves, diced
1 large carrot, cut into chunky cubes
1 large potato, peeled and cut into 2cm cubes
300g chestnut mushrooms, sliced
1 x 400ml can coconut milk
1 tsp freshly ground black pepper
1 tsp ground pimento (allspice)
3–4 basil leaves
1 tsp dried thyme
80g okra, halved lengthways
Salt

Curries and Stews

Trini split pea dhal with spinach and okra

Serves 4

Trinidad is known for its special dhal dishes. With a massive Indian influence on the island, they have created some of the best veggie curries, and you're getting just that here. We've added mango chutney, spinach and okra to give that EXTRA FLAVA!

It's best to soak the peas for a few hours or overnight to plump them up a bit, but it's not necessary if you don't have time.

Firstly, wash and drain the split peas two or three times, until the water runs clear. Add them to a large pot with the water and bring to the boil. Now season di ting with the onion, scotch bonnet, turmeric, ground cumin, pimento, mango chutney and salt and black pepper to taste. Simmer for 40 minutes until the peas are tender.

Use a stick blender to blend until mushy but not completely smooth. Add a likkle more salt and black pepper to taste, stir in the spinach to wilt, take off the heat and allow to rest – the liquid will soak into the peas, thickening it. Add a little more hot water if it needs loosening.

In a frying pan, heat the oil and add the garlic, cumin seeds and bay leaves. Fry for 3–4 minutes until sizzling and fragrant, being careful not to burn them, then dash them into the curry.

In the same frying pan, pan-fry the sliced okra and serve alongside the curry, with rice and flatbreads. Serve extra mango chutney and hot pepper sauce on the side.

350g dried split peas
1.7 litres water
1 medium onion, very finely chopped
1 scotch bonnet pepper, deseeded and very finely chopped
2 tbsp ground turmeric
1 tsp ground cumin
1 tsp ground pimento (allspice)
1 tbsp mango chutney, plus extra to serve
Handful of spinach
3 tbsp vegetable oil
4 garlic cloves, chopped
1 tbsp cumin seeds
2 bay leaves
8 okra, sliced lengthways
Salt and freshly ground black pepper

Plantain and bean stew

Serves 4

We love stew! Mum and Nan always made stews when we were younger, and it was a meal that fed the whole family on a budget at the end of the week. The flavas always taste amazing because of the spices, but also – especially – because of the love that was put into the meal. We always had plantain and beans in the kitchen, so this was made often. Sweet flava from the plantain and dense nutty flava from the beans. Yeahh mon! The ting good!

Heat the coconut oil in a pot over a medium heat, add the spring onions, garlic, scotch bonnet, celery and carrots and cook for 3–4 minutes until caramelised. Stir in the kidney beans and plantain, then crumble in the stock cubes and tip in the tomatoes and water. Bring to the boil, add the thyme sprigs and season with salt and black pepper to taste. Simmer for 10 minutes until the plantain is cooked.

Sprinkle with the chopped parsley, if you like, and serve with quinoa or brown rice.

1 tbsp coconut oil
2 spring onions, sliced
2 garlic cloves, diced
½ scotch bonnet pepper, deseeded and finely chopped
2 celery sticks, diced
2 carrots, diced
1 x 400g can kidney beans, drained and rinsed
2 unripe plantain, peeled and sliced
2 vegan stock cubes
1 x 400g can plum tomatoes
250ml water
4–6 fresh thyme sprigs
Salt and freshly ground black pepper
Fresh parsley, chopped, to serve (optional)

Curries and Stews

Brown stew broccoli

Serves 4

This is a great way to get your five-a-day veggies in! Tender veggies stewed in a thick browning sauce with so much FLAVA. It's a really simple recipe to put together, especially good for after a long day's work.

This is delicious with sides like rice, bulgur wheat or even with some noodles or pasta, but it's very versatile and can be eaten with most dishes. We've taken inspiration from the Jamaican stew chicken method, and used plump vegetables as an alternative, and there's no better plump vegetables than broccoli and mushrooms! They soak up the flavours, which makes it a warm and comforting dish you'll love.

Put the broccoli and mushrooms in a mixing bowl, add the pimento, smoked paprika, browning, salt and black pepper, then mix together and set aside.

Mix all the browning ingredients together until combined.

Heat the oil in a large frying pan over a medium heat, add the onion and garlic and cook down for 5–7 minutes until soft. Add the bell pepper, scotch bonnet and thyme, then stir in the browning mixture. Add the broccoli and mushrooms and stir. Cook for 20 minutes until the veggies are cooked.

1 medium head of broccoli, cut into florets
200g chestnut mushrooms, sliced
½ tsp ground pimento (allspice)
¼ tsp smoked paprika
1 tsp browning or 1 tbsp dark soy sauce
1 tsp salt
1 tsp freshly ground black pepper
2 tbsp olive oil
1 medium onion, diced
1 garlic clove, very finely chopped
1 red bell pepper, deseeded and cut into fine strips
¼ scotch bonnet pepper, diced
1 tbsp chopped fresh thyme leaves

For the browning
2 tbsp olive oil
1½ tsp browning or 1½ tbsp dark soy sauce
1 tbsp tomato purée
250ml vegan stock or water
2 tbsp tomato ketchup
2 tsp vegan butter

Ital stew

Ital is vital! And you'll find out why after you nyamed pon dis plate right here! Hearty vegetables are a staple part of Ital eating, along with stews filled with the most authentic flavours.

We call this 'hard food' in the Caribbean, because it uses starchy veg that give you energy and provide great fibre. Usain is known to attribute his speed and strength to hard food!

So if you want to be like Bolt – eat this.

Heat the oil in a large pot over a medium heat, add the onion, garlic, carrots, celery and spring onions and cook down for 5–7 minutes until caramelised.

Stir in the thyme, pumpkin, plantain, tomatoes and lentils and cook for 5–10 minutes, to add some colour to the pumpkin. Add the pimento and season with salt and black pepper.

Crumble in the stock cubes, then add the coconut milk and a likkle water (enough so the liquid covers the veg). Cook for 20 minutes until the veggies are fully cooked.

Serve with bulgur wheat and peas (see page 204), green banana and cornmeal dumplings (see page 65).

2 tbsp olive oil
1 red onion, chopped
4 garlic cloves, chopped
2 carrots, chopped
2 celery sticks, chopped
2 spring onions, chopped
3–4 fresh thyme springs
175g pumpkin or butternut squash, peeled, deseeded and cut into bite-sized chunks
1 ripe plantain, peeled and sliced
2 medium tomatoes, chopped
1 x 400g can lentils, drained
1 tsp ground pimento (allspice)
2 vegan stock cubes
1 x 400ml can coconut milk
120g sliced greens (any leafy greens)
Salt and coarsely ground black pepper

Chickpea and potato curry with buss up shut roti

Serves 4–6

Known as chana and aloo in Trinidad, this curry is a blend of fragrant spices in a rich base, with potato and chickpeas softened and mashed down to add extra thickness. It really is a unique way to add extra volume to a curry, and we love it. Our favourite way to eat it is with roti – either wrapped in one or dipping buss up shut roti into it – and enjoy the excess that drops on the fingers too! We also love to serve it with mashed pumpkin and a fresh cucumber chutney (grated cucumber, chopped chilli and a dash of lime juice) on the side.

Rich with flavour and history, this curry is enjoyed by Caribbeans from street corners, and especially after a carnival party! So bring the Trini good feeling to your kitchen with this sure-to-be favourite!

In a large pan, heat the oil over a medium heat, then add the cumin seeds and stir for 20 seconds. Add the onion, garlic, scotch bonnet and half the curry powder and cook for 2–3 minutes until softened.

Add the thyme sprigs, coriander and spring onions and cook down for a further 2 minutes. Stir in the remaining curry powder, the turmeric and grated ginger and cook for 1 minute, then add a likkle water and combine all the ingredients together.

Fling in the potatoes and mix around until they are coated in the spices. Add the chickpeas and stir to coat in the same way. Add the water, dash in salt and black pepper to taste and simmer until the potatoes are tender.

Once the potatoes have softened, press down on some of them, and on some chickpeas (not all of them); this adds thickness to the sauce. If it looks too thick, add a little more water.

And ya dun! Serve with the buss up shut rotis, and for extra flava, we like to serve with mango chutney too; it gives it a nice, fruity bounce.

2 tbsp vegetable oil
1 tsp cumin seeds
1 onion, diced
3 garlic cloves, finely chopped
½ scotch bonnet pepper, deseeded and diced
2 tbsp Caribbean curry powder
4 fresh thyme sprigs
Small handful of coriander leaves, finely chopped
2 spring onions, chopped
1 tbsp ground turmeric
3cm piece of fresh ginger, grated
4 medium potatoes, peeled and chopped into 2cm cubes
2 x 400g cans chickpeas, drained and rinsed
500ml water
Salt and freshly ground black pepper

To serve
4–6 buss up shut rotis (see page 194)
1 tbsp mango chutney (optional)

Root vegetable stew with dumplings

Serves 4–5

A warm, hearty stew with a whole heap of flava. And hench dumplings too! Growing up, stews were something we had regularly, especially living in the UK as it was always cold. The spices in this dish create a volcano of deliciousness.

Make the dumplings by mixing the flour, salt and butter together in a bowl, rubbing the butter in with your fingertips. Add enough water to bring it together into a smooth dough, knead briefly then cover and set aside in the fridge to rest for 10 minutes.

Meanwhile, heat the oil in a large pot over a medium heat, add the onion, garlic and spring onions and cook down for about 5 minutes until soft.

Add the pumpkin or squash, yam and carrots and cook for 5 minutes, then stir in the stock. Season with the black pepper and add the pimento, thyme sprigs, scotch bonnet and bay leaves. Bring to the boil and allow to bubble gently for about 20 minutes until the vegetables are soft. Add the cornflour paste and stir to thicken.

Divide the dumpling dough into 5 and shape each into a ball. Add to the stew then cover and simmer for 15 minutes. Remove the scotch bonnet before serving.

For the dumplings
175g self-raising flour
Pinch of salt
60g vegan butter, softened
About 100ml water

For the stew
2 tbsp vegetable oil
1 medium onion, chopped
4 garlic cloves, chopped
2 spring onions, chopped
1 small pumpkin or butternut squash (about 400g), peeled, deseeded and cut into 2cm cubes
1 white or yellow yam (or about 400g sweet or white potatoes), peeled and cut into 2cm cubes
2 carrots, sliced
500ml vegan stock
1 tsp freshly ground black pepper
1 tsp ground pimento (allspice)
4 fresh thyme sprigs
1 scotch bonnet pepper
2 bay leaves
1 tsp cornflour mixed to a paste with a likkle water

Jackfruit rundown

We absolutely love jackfruit – such a delicious fruit that absorbs flavours so well! And since it has a similar flaky structure to fish we've used it to create a vegan version of a Jamaican favourite, mackerel rundown. Cooked down in a tasty coconut and tomato sauce with Caribbean spices, it will have you licking every drop off your plate!

Canned jackfruit is easily available nowadays, and you should be able to find it at your local supermarket or African or Caribbean store.

We 100% recommend eating this dish with boiled green banana and cornmeal dumplings (see page 65), so you can use them to sweep up the sauce. Ah, just thinking about it is making our bellies rumble!

Bring a small pan of water to the boil. Add the jackfruit and simmer for 5–7 minutes until soft, then drain and use a fork to pull into shreds. Set aside.

Heat the coconut oil in a large frying pan over a medium heat, add the onion, garlic, spring onions and bell pepper and cook down for 5–7 minutes until caramelised. Add the coconut milk, mix and bring to the boil, then simmer for 3–4 minutes.

Add the jackfruit, tomato, thyme sprigs and scotch bonnet, then add the pimento and curry powder and season with salt and black pepper to taste. Mix together and cook for 5 minutes, then lower the heat and simmer for a further 5 minutes.

Serve with green banana and boiled dumplings.

1 x 560g can young green jackfruit in brine, drained and rinsed
2 tbsp coconut oil
1 small onion, sliced
2 garlic cloves, chopped
2 spring onions, sliced
1 red bell pepper, deseeded and cut into thin strips
1 x 400ml can coconut milk
1 large tomato, chopped
3 fresh thyme sprigs
¼ scotch bonnet pepper, deseeded and diced
1 tsp ground pimento (allspice)
½ tsp curry powder
Salt and freshly ground black pepper

No-bully-beef stew

A plant-based version of corn beef stew, aka bully beef stew. We cook this the same way we used to cook bully beef; it has a similar taste and looks identical, but this is a healthier, lighter version, and you won't miss the beef!

Heat the oil in a frying pan over a medium heat, add the onion, garlic, bell pepper and thyme, then cook down for 5–7 minutes until soft.

Add the mince and cook down, stirring, to add colour and break it up, then add the pimento and season with salt and black pepper to taste. Stir in the tomato purée and water and cook for 10 minutes, adding a likkle more water if it turns too dry.

Finally, throw in the sweetcorn and simmer for 5 minutes before serving, with rice or fried dumplings.

2 tbsp olive oil
1 small onion, sliced
4 garlic cloves, chopped
1 red bell pepper, deseeded
   and sliced
3–4 fresh thyme sprigs
300g meat-free mince
1 tsp ground pimento (allspice)
4 tbsp tomato purée
125ml water
100g drained, canned sweetcorn
Salt and coarsely ground
   black pepper

Family and Sharing Flava   132

As brothers of Caribbean descent, food (and lots of it) was, is and will always be a vital part of our lives, especially when it comes to get-togethers with family and friends. So we've filled this chapter with big portions and bigger flavas that are sure to bring smiles to all those faces.

Food is the party starter: having great food on the table is integral to an unforgettable time! Usually there'd be a meat centrepiece, but those have now met their match with our vegan creations, such as jerk-spiced Wellington, a massive sharing patty, chilli con carne and shepherd's pie.

We've got something for all occasions, whether you want to impress your vegan in-laws, or are having a few meat-eating friends over and want to show them this vegan ting is niceee still! We got you!

And not forgetting the bubbling veggie soups we have – it's time to get everyone over and make use of that big fancy oven dish or pot you got for Christmas!

Spiced pepper nuts

Makes 25 servings

Growing up, we used to go to lots of family gatherings, and most weekends we were at some sort of party with our parents. And roasted nuts would always be there as an easy snack while waiting for the main feast. Our mum loves them too, so we decided to add our own spicy spin.

Melt the butter in a large frying pan, add the garlic and scotch bonnet and cook down for 2 minutes, then add in the mixed nuts and cook, stirring, until toasted. Add the curry powder, paprika and salt to taste, mix and tip into a bowl to cool before serving.

Store roasted nuts in an airtight container in a cool dark place. Eat within 2 weeks.

2 tbsp vegan butter
1 tsp very finely chopped garlic
½ scotch bonnet pepper, deseeded and very finely chopped
750g mixed nuts (peanuts, walnuts, pecans, cashews)
¼ tsp curry powder
1 tsp cayenne pepper or paprika
Flaky sea salt

Family and Sharing Flava   137

Ital pumpkin sip sip soup

Serves 6–8

A soup taken from the Jamaican Rastafarian Ital way of living – no additives, food straight from the earth – offering an abundance of nutritional benefits for the body and flavour that is good for the soul!

The key to getting the best out of this soup is to take your time with it: let the starchy and fragrant vegetables break down and melt into the broth. Ya mon, dis one is a must during the cold winter months.

Bring the water to the boil in a large pot, add the pumpkin, yam, dasheen, if using, onion, garlic, spring onions, ginger, pimento, and salt and black pepper to taste, and let it boil up for about 15 minutes. This will allow the harder vegetables to soften up and the fragrant veggies to release the flavour into the base of the soup.

Add the carrots and corn on the cob and boil for another 10 minutes, then add the greens, scotch bonnet and thyme and simmer for a final 5 minutes.

Remove the scotch bonnet and it's done!

1.5 litres water
750g pumpkin or butternut squash, peeled, deseeded and diced
200g white or yellow yam, peeled and diced
200g yellow dasheen (optional)
1 onion, chopped
6 garlic cloves, chopped
2 spring onions, chopped
5cm piece of fresh ginger, peeled and grated
8 pimento (allspice) berries
3 carrots, chopped
2 corn on the cob, sliced into chunky sections
200g spring greens, roughly chopped into short lengths
1 scotch bonnet pepper
10 fresh thyme sprigs
Salt and freshly ground black pepper

Caribbean corn soup

This dish is inspired by Trini corn soup, but we added our twist to it. It's full of so much flavour – one of those dishes that as soon as it hits your tongue you go ahhhh. Perfect for those cold weekends indoors, and it goes really well with a piece of warm bread, too, or make the dumplings on page 141 and add to the soup for the last 5 minutes.

It's a blend of blitzed and whole pieces of corn, which gives a great texture and flavour too. There's something so feel-good about munching on a corn cob in a big ol' soup!

Heat the oil in a large pot over a medium heat, add the onion, garlic, chopped scotch bonnet, spring onions, celery, chives and thyme and cook down for 5–7 minutes until the onion softens.

Add the pumpkin, split peas, canned sweetcorn, potatoes and half the carrots, then add the water (making sure it covers the veg; if not, add a little more) and crumble in the stock cube. Add salt and black pepper to taste, bring to the boil, then simmer for about 30 minutes, stirring occasionally.

Add the coconut milk then use a stick blender to blitz until smooth. Add the corn on the cob pieces, remaining carrots and green seasoning, if using, and bring back to the boil. If you like extra spice, add the whole scotch bonnet, then simmer for 15 minutes, removing the whole scotch bonnet just before serving.

2 tbsp vegetable oil
1 onion, chopped
2 garlic cloves, chopped
½ scotch bonnet pepper, deseeded and chopped, plus an extra (optional) whole scotch bonnet
2 spring onions, chopped
1 celery stick, chopped
4–6 chives, chopped
1 tsp dried thyme
200g pumpkin, peeled, deseeded and diced
50g split peas
1 x 340g can sweetcorn, drained
2 medium potatoes, peeled and chopped
4 carrots, chopped
700ml water
1 vegan stock cube
1 x 400ml can coconut milk
2 corn on the cob, sliced into chunky sections
1 tsp green seasoning (see page 102), optional
Salt and freshly ground black pepper

Red pea soup

We just love going back to Jamaica, and one of the main reasons is the easy and FREE access to the wonderful vegetables that are just so great to cook with, especially in soups. Thankfully they are in most supermarkets and veg markets over here these days, so you too can enjoy these super-easy and hearty soups.

The flavours in this soup are an absolute joy. You will love it, and it's full of fantastic root vegetables that have endless nutritional benefits. Inspired by the Rasta Ital diet, this soup will make you feel irieee!

Bring the water to the boil in a large pot. Add the kidney beans, pumpkin or squash, yam, dasheen, cho cho, carrots, ginger, thyme, pimento berries, ground pimento and salt and black pepper to taste. Stir, cover and boil it down for 20 minutes.

Meanwhile, for the dumplings, mix the flour, cornmeal and salt in a bowl. Add enough water to make a dough, knead briefly until smooth, then set aside to rest for 5 minutes.

Add the coconut milk to the soup and stir. Tear small pieces off the dough and roll into mini dumplings (or long, thin shapes known as spinners) and dash them into the soup with the scotch bonnet. Cover and simmer for 10 minutes, then add the greens and simmer for a final 5 minutes.

Remove the scotch bonnet, then the ting done and ready to nyam!

1.5 litres water
2 x 400g cans kidney beans, drained and rinsed
500g peeled, deseeded and cubed pumpkin or butternut squash
200g white or yellow yam, peeled and cubed
200g dasheen (or yam or potato), chopped
1 cho cho (chayote), peeled and chopped
3 carrots, thickly sliced
5cm piece of fresh ginger, peeled and grated
6 fresh thyme sprigs
8 pimento (allspice) berries
½ tsp ground pimento (allspice)
1 x 400ml can coconut milk
1 scotch bonnet pepper
200g spring greens
Salt and freshly ground black pepper

For the dumplings/spinners
250g plain flour
1 tbsp coarse cornmeal
½ tsp salt
About 150ml water

Pepper pot soup

A vegan version of a Caribbean favourite – the traditional version is filled with different meats, but we've stripped it back with this fresh, flavour-filled, plant-based version.

The star of the show is fresh callaloo, which we know can be hard to find in some areas, so use spinach, greens or kale instead, rather than canned greens.

Heat the coconut oil in a large pot over a medium heat, add the onion, chopped scotch bonnet, bay leaves, spring onions, thyme, garlic and ginger, and cook down for 5–7 minutes until softened. Add the pumpkin, yam, potatoes, carrots, pimento and salt and black pepper to taste. Stir in half the callaloo, the stock and coconut milk, bring to the boil, then simmer for 20 minutes.

Add the dumpling spinners and whole scotch bonnet, if using, and simmer for 10 minutes before adding the remaining callaloo and the okra. Simmer for a final 5 minutes, removing the whole scotch bonnet before serving.

2 tsp coconut oil
1 small onion, finely chopped
1 scotch bonnet pepper, deseeded and finely chopped, plus an extra (optional) whole scotch bonnet
2 bay leaves
2 spring onions, chopped
6 fresh thyme sprigs
3 garlic cloves, crushed
3cm piece of fresh ginger, peeled and grated
350g pumpkin, peeled, deseeded and chopped
200g white or yellow yam, peeled and chopped
350g potatoes and sweet potatoes (50/50), peeled and chopped
2 carrots, chopped
5 pimento (allspice) berries or 1 tsp ground allspice
400g fresh callaloo (or spinach, fresh greens or kale), roughly chopped
750ml vegan stock
1 x 400ml can coconut milk
1 x quantity dumpling spinners (see page 141)
6 okra, halved
Salt and freshly ground black pepper

Plantain and spinach lasagne

Serves 6–8

This is not your traditional lasagne, this is one with NUFF FLAVA! It's inspired by the Caribbean and Puerto Rican layered casserole dish called pastelón that usually uses minced beef.

The dish has a different style across the Caribbean islands, so we've put our vegan spin on it – Original Flava style! Layers of sweet plantain, spinach and vegan mozzarella to give a real cheesy and golden topping. The taste is out of this world, and is a real crowd-pleaser too!

Preheat the oven to 180°C Fan/200°C/Gas 6.

Peel the plantain and slice each lengthways into 3 strips. Heat enough oil for shallow-frying in a large frying pan, add the plantain strips and fry over a medium-high heat for 3–4 minutes on each side until golden brown, then remove to a tray lined with kitchen paper, to drain excess oil.

For the filling, use the same frying pan, tipping out most of the cooking oil. Add the onion and garlic and sauté over a medium heat until soft. Add the mince and cook, stirring, for about 5 minutes until browned, then add the scotch bonnet and salt and pepper to taste, and cook for a further 5 minutes. Tip into a bowl and wipe out the frying pan.

For the tomato sauce, heat the olive oil in the same pan over a medium heat, add the onion and garlic and cook over for 5 minutes over a medium heat to caramelise. Add the chopped tomatoes and cook for 5 minutes, season with salt and black pepper, add the dried basil and cook for 15 minutes over a low heat. Stir in the fresh basil and remove from the heat.

For the cheese sauce, heat the oil in a separate pan, add the flour and cook, stirring, for a minute or two. Gradually add the milk, whisking to incorporate it after each addition. When all the milk is absorbed and you have a smooth sauce, simmer for 2–3 minutes, then add the cheese and stir to mix. Remove from the heat.

3–4 ripe plantain
Vegetable oil, for shallow-frying
1 medium onion, diced
4 garlic cloves, diced
600g meat-free mince
½ scotch bonnet pepper, deseeded and diced
2 handfuls of fresh spinach
300g grated vegan mozzarella-style cheese
Salt and freshly ground black pepper

For the tomato sauce
2 tbsp olive oil
1 small onion, diced
2 garlic cloves, diced
200g canned chopped tomatoes
1 tsp dried basil
1 tbsp basil leaves, chopped

For the cheese sauce
3 tbsp vegetable oil
2½ tbsp plain flour
500ml plant-based milk of your choice
100g grated vegan cheese

Add 4–6 teaspoons of tomato sauce to the base of a lasagne dish, about 30 x 21cm and 7cm deep, then spread 6–8 tablespoons of mince mixture across the top followed by the spinach and a third of the grated cheese. Add plantain slices on top to cover the whole area (trimming them to fit if necessary). Now add more mince on top and scatter over another third of the cheese. Add another layer of plantain, then the rest of the tomato sauce in between the plantain. Finally, pour the cheese sauce over the top, sprinkle over the remaining grated cheese and bake for 25 minutes until golden and bubbling.

Family and Sharing Flava

Family and Sharing Flava   146

Escovitch tofish

Easter is one of our favourite times of the year. It's a time when our family comes together to cook and eat lots of incredible food! Similar to most Caribbean households, fish in its many forms is served at this time: escovitched, stewed, fried, jerked... the list goes on.

So we wanted to create a version of escovitch fish for vegans, using the same techniques, with all the flava of course, but with plant-based ingredients. So we have a delicious crunchy fried tofu with a cooked-down escovitch dressing. At Easter, we would serve this with fried dumpling, bammy, breadfruit, steamed cabbage and water crackers.

First, prepare your tofu. After draining off any water in the packet, place a plate on top of the block of tofu and press down on it for 30 seconds, then blot with kitchen paper to remove as much water as you can. Cut the tofu into equal 4 slices, add to a mixing bowl and season with the seaweed seasoning, if using, and salt and black pepper to taste. Add the coconut milk and mix together.

Heat enough vegetable oil for shallow-frying in a large frying pan over a medium-high heat. While the oil is heating, mix the flour, cornflour, paprika and curry powder together in a bowl.

Remove the tofu slices from the coconut mixture, gently shaking off any excess liquid, then dip to coat all over in the dry mixture. Repeat to double-coat each slice. Transfer to the hot oil and cook for 2–3 minutes on each side until golden. Remove to a plate lined with kitchen paper, to absorb excess oil, and keep warm.

Heat a glug of oil in a clean or separate frying pan and add the bell peppers, onion, carrot, vinegar and salt and black pepper to taste. Cook down, stirring, until soft. Serve the tofish with the dressing, lemon wedges for squeezing over, and some hard-dough bread on the side.

1 x 420g block of firm tofu
1 tsp seaweed seasoning (dried seaweed flakes), optional
125ml coconut milk
Vegetable oil, for shallow-frying
50g plain flour
2 tbsp cornflour
1 tsp paprika
1 tsp curry powder
Salt and freshly ground black pepper
1 lemon, cut into wedges, to serve

For the escovitch dressing
1 red bell pepper, deseeded and cut into julienne
1 yellow bell pepper, deseeded and cut into julienne
1 medium onion, thinly sliced
1 carrot, cut into julienne
1 tbsp white vinegar

Family and Sharing Flava 149

Vegan shepherd's pie

Serves 6

We've put our own little Caribbean spin on a dish we loved when we were growing up because it was so hearty and flavaful, making it really natural by using lots of plant-based ingredients.

If you are wondering what to do with all those vegetables in your fridge, we've got the perfect recipe to save the day! No one likes waste – just like Nan says, don't budda waste no food mon. She'll love us giving her a big up!

Preheat the oven to 190°C Fan/210°C/Gas 7.

Cook the potatoes in a pan of boiling, salted water until tender.

Meanwhile, heat the oil in a large frying pan over a medium heat, add the onion and garlic and cook down for 5–7 minutes until soft. Mix in 300ml of the coconut milk, then add the tomatoes, stock granules, carrots, peas, if using, and thyme. Stir through the chickpeas and lentils. Season with salt and black pepper, add the water and browning, if using, and cook it all down for 5–7 minutes.

Drain the potatoes, return them to the pan and mash down until smooth, then add the remaining coconut milk along with the butter. Add salt to taste and mix until well combined.

Tip the chickpea and lentil mixture into an ovenproof dish. Spoon the mashed potato on top and spread it into an even layer. Use a fork to create a textured surface, and bake in the oven for 30 minutes until bubbling underneath and golden on top.

6 large potatoes, peeled and quartered
1 tbsp olive oil
1 medium onion, finely chopped
2 garlic cloves, very finely chopped
1 x 400ml can coconut milk
3 large tomatoes, diced
2 tbsp vegan stock granules
2 medium carrots, diced
200g frozen peas (optional)
1 tsp dried thyme
1 tsp all-purpose seasoning
1 x 400g can chickpeas, drained and rinsed
2 x 400g cans of lentils, drained
150ml water
1 tsp browning or 1 tbsp dark soy sauce (optional)
6 tbsp vegan butter
Salt and freshly ground black pepper

Family and Sharing Flava

Sweet potato and callaloo pie

Serves 6–8

This pie is absolutely flavalicious! A dish that will warm your belly and bring nuff joy to it too. The creamy sweetness of the topping and the glorious spicy callaloo underneath will bring your taste buds so much excitement!

This is really easy to make, and is family friendly too. Serve with some crunchy salad and a thick gravy.

Preheat the oven to 180ºC Fan/200ºC/Gas 6.

Cook the sweet potatoes in a pot of boiling water until soft.

Meanwhile, grab a frying pan and heat the oil over a medium-high heat. Add the onion, garlic and scotch bonnet and sauté for a few minutes. Add the bell peppers and tomatoes, along with half the pimento, thyme and paprika. Mix together, add salt and black pepper to taste, then stir in the peas and callaloo or spinach and simmer for 5–7 minutes until soft. Tip into an ovenproof dish, about 23 x 33cm, and level it out.

Drain your sweet potatoes and return them to the pan with the butter. Mash down until smooth, add a sprinkling of black pepper and the remaining pimento, thyme and paprika and mix together.

Spoon the mashed sweet potato on top of the filling, spread it out evenly and sprinkle with thyme and black pepper on top. Bake in the oven for 40 minutes until golden on top and bubbling underneath.

6 sweet potatoes, peeled and cut into chunks
1 tbsp vegetable oil
1 medium onion, diced
4 garlic cloves, diced
1 scotch bonnet pepper, deseeded and diced
½ red bell pepper, deseeded and diced
½ green bell pepper, deseeded and diced
2 large tomatoes, diced
2 tsp ground pimento (allspice)
2 tsp dried thyme, plus extra to sprinkle
2 tsp paprika
200g frozen peas
1 x 540g can callaloo, drained, or 280g fresh spinach, chopped
2 tbsp vegan butter
Salt and freshly ground black pepper

Lentil nut roast

Our mum is a vegan and this is her nut roast, a favourite dish for special occasions like Mother's Day or as a centrepiece on a family Sunday dinner table. We've grown up with such occasions, where there's a big dish bang in the centre of the table to be shared around.

Dash some thick gravy pon top for a really indulgent meal. It's packed full of flava and freshness!

Line a 900g/2lb loaf tin with baking parchment, making sure there is enough overhang on the long sides to be able to lift out the nut roast when baked.

In a small bowl, mix the chia seeds with the warm water and leave for 10–15 minutes until it becomes a thick paste.

Meanwhile, heat the oil in a large frying pan over a medium heat, add the onion, garlic, carrot, celery, bell peppers and scotch bonnet. Cook for 5 minutes, then add the mushrooms and lentils, dash in the paprika, ginger, all-purpose seasoning and salt and black pepper to taste, and cook for 5–7 minutes until soft. Set aside to cool completely.

Preheat the oven to 170ºC Fan/190ºC/Gas 5.

Combine the breadcumbs, stuffing mix, nuts and dried fruit in a large mixing bowl. Add the soaked chia seeds, then add your cooked vegetables and mix everything together until fully combined. Tip the mixture into the lined loaf tin, pack it down gently and bake in the oven for 1 hour until slightly browned on top.

Remove from the oven and lift out onto a board. Cut into slices to serve.

2 tbsp chia seeds
3 tbsp warm water
2 tbsp olive oil
1 onion, diced
2 garlic cloves, diced
1 carrot, diced
1 celery stick, diced
½ red bell pepper, deseeded and diced
1 orange bell pepper, deseeded and diced
1 scotch bonnet pepper, deseeded and diced
4 medium mushrooms, diced
1 x 400g can green lentils, drained and rinsed
1 tbsp paprika
1 tsp ground ginger
1 tbsp all-purpose seasoning
100g breadcrumbs
1 x 170g packet sage and onion stuffing mix (Paxo brand)
50g mixed nuts (such as almonds, walnuts etc), chopped
50g dried fruit (such as currants, raisins, etc)
Salt and freshly ground black pepper

Giant patty

You definitely need this on the dinner table when the family or friends come over. Giant patty! Sounds good, eh. Jamaican patties are one the most popular snacks on the island, often made with beef, chicken or fish. With plant-based food being so accessible these days, there are a variety of meat substitutes, such as meat-free mince. All you have to do is add some flava and you'll be able to create a lighter and FLAVAFUL substitute. Serve as it is, or with some coleslaw.

For the pastry, sift the flour into a bowl, then stir in the sugar, salt and turmeric. Add the butter and shortening and rub them into the dry ingredients using your fingertips, until you have a crumbly texture. Gradually add enough of the ice-cold water to create a dough. Form the dough into a ball, wrap in cling film and chill in the fridge for 1 hour.

Meanwhile, for the filling, heat the oil in a frying pan over a medium heat, add the onion, garlic, scotch bonnet and mushrooms and cook for a few minutes. Add the mince and cook, stirring, until browned all over, then stir in the black pepper and pimento. Add the stock, keeping back 1 tablespoon, then add the browning. Mix the reserved stock into the cornflour to make a paste, add to the pan, stir well and cook for 10–12 minutes until thickened. Set aside to cool.

Preheat the oven to 180°C Fan/200°C/Gas 6.

Take the chilled pastry dough out of the fridge. Dust the work surface with a little flour, then roll out the dough using a rolling pin into a large round, about the thickness of a pound coin. Invert a large mixing bowl, about 30cm in diameter, over the pastry, and use a sharp knife to cut around it to create a neat round. Add the cooled filling to the centre of the round. Brush a likkle bit of almond milk around the edges of the pastry and fold the pastry over into a big half-moon shape, pressing the edges together to seal. Use a fork to crimp the edges, and then prick a few steam holes in the centre.

Carefully transfer to a baking tray, brush the top of the patty with almond milk and bake in the oven for 30–35 minutes until the pastry is evenly cooked and golden.

For the pastry
450g self-raising flour, plus extra for dusting
2 tsp brown sugar
1 tsp salt
3 tbsp ground turmeric
30g chilled vegan butter, diced
30g chilled vegan shortening or lard, diced
About 200ml ice-cold water
Almond milk, for brushing

For the filling
1 tbsp vegetable oil
1 medium onion, diced
4 garlic cloves, diced
1 scotch bonnet pepper, deseeded and diced
150g chestnut mushrooms, finely chopped
250g meat-free mince
¼ tsp freshly ground black pepper
1½ tsp ground pimento (allspice)
1 vegan stock cube, mixed with 250ml boiling water
½ tsp browning or 1½ tsp dark soy sauce
½ tbsp cornflour

Jerk-spiced squash and callaloo Wellington

Serves 6–8

Here we transfer the jerk method usually used on meat to create a spicy jerk-flavoured sweet squash covered with delicious puff pastry! Mmmmm, sounds like heaven. This is the perfect recipe to have on the dinner table with family and friends. Get ready for the FLAVA.

Preheat the oven 200°C Fan/220°C/Gas 7.

Cut the long neck end off each squash (save the seedy end for another use). Peel, place on a baking tray and coat in the jerk seasoning to cover them evenly. Roast in the oven for about 45 minutes until just tender (not too soft, as it will cook longer in the pastry). Remove and set aside to cool completely.

Meanwhile, for the filling, heat the oil in a large frying pan over a medium heat, add the onion, garlic and spring onions and cook down until caramelised. Add the mushrooms and cook for a few minutes until browned. Season with the salt, black pepper and pimento, and mix together. Add the wine, if using, and callaloo or spinach, mix and cook down for 10 minutes until the liquid has evaporated and the mixture is quite dry. Set aside to cool completely.

Place one pastry sheet on a baking sheet, trimming it to about 28 x 23cm if necessary. Sprinkle over the breadcrumbs then spread over a layer of cooled filling, leaving a clear pastry border around the edges, then sit the squash necks end to end down the middle of the filling. Brush the jerk BBQ sauce all over the squash, then pack the remaining filling around the squash.

Brush a little almond milk around the clear borders of the pastry and place the second pastry sheet on top. Use your hands to gently press it around the squash and down to meet the bottom pastry sheet. Press the edges together, trim all around to make a neat edge, then use a fork to crimp and seal.

Brush almond milk all over the pastry, make a few steam holes in the top using a small, sharp knife, and bake in the oven for 25–30 minutes until golden brown. Cut into thick slices to serve.

2 butternut squash
1 tbsp jerk seasoning (see page 166)
2 x 320g vegan puff pastry sheets
3 tbsp jerk BBQ sauce (see page 166 for homemade)
Almond milk, for brushing

For the filling
1 tbsp vegetable oil
1 white onion, diced
4 garlic cloves, diced
2 spring onions, sliced
500g chestnut mushrooms, diced
½ tsp salt
½ tsp freshly ground black pepper
½ tsp ground pimento (allspice)
30ml Red Label wine or red wine (ensure vegan), optional
300g fresh callaloo or spinach
40g breadcrumbs

Caribbean chilli con carne

The Caribbean is blessed with amazing beans and peas which we usually use for rice and stews. Growing up in the UK, chilli con carne was a dish that was very popular, so now we've created a meatless version that is full of flava.

Heat the oil in a pan over a medium heat, add the onion and garlic and cook for 7–10 minutes until caramelised. Add the bell pepper and cook until soft, then add the mince and cook, stirring, for 5 minutes.

Add the beans, tomatoes and tomato purée, then crumble in the stock cube and add 250ml of water. Add the chilli powder, pimento, all-purpose seasoning and scotch bonnet, season with salt and black pepper to taste, cover and cook for 10 minutes, until well combined and aromatic.

Serve with brown rice.

2 tbsp olive oil
1 large onion, diced
4 garlic cloves, chopped
1 red bell pepper, deseeded and diced
300g meat-free mince
1 x 400g can Caribbean mixed beans, or kidney beans, drained and rinsed
1 x 400g can chopped tomatoes
1 tbsp tomato purée
1 vegan stock cube
1 tsp chilli powder
1 tsp ground pimento (allspice)
1 tsp all-purpose seasoning
1 scotch bonnet pepper, deseeded and finely chopped (or extra chilli powder)
Salt and freshly ground black pepper

Family and Sharing Flava   159

FIRED UP

FLAVA

Yes! You can jerk vegetables. It's not just for meats. The fundamentals of jerk are the smoking and seasoning processes. And you can most definitely use these on your vegetables. Our nan does an annual BBQ for her birthday, and we are in charge of getting the party started with some jerk – and rum of course! And we love to explore different and exciting ways to jerk vegetables and fruit.

How many times have you gone to a BBQ and the only vegan option is a packet of leafy salad no one has opened? We are here to bring an end to that, with a whole lot of dishes to feast pon!

In this chapter you'll find inspiration to create the ultimate jerk BBQ feast. There's a jerk fruit platter, jerk-spiced lentil burger, jerk Portobello mushroom wrap, grilled chilli corn... with some delicious sides and salads you'll want alongside it all.

So grab your jerk pan or barbecue grill (although most recipes can be done in the oven too), your cold beers and rum punch and get ready for a FLAVAFUL vegan summer party!

Fired Up Flava

Jerk seasoning

Makes about 12 tablespoons

Give your vegetables that traditional dry jerk rub to enhance the flavour, with this blend of spices to make the ultimate jerk seasoning from scratch. Store in an airtight jar and it will last a long time.

2 tbsp onion powder
2 tbsp garlic powder
2 tsp cayenne pepper
2 tsp paprika
2 tbsp ground pimento (allspice)
2 tsp salt
2 tsp coarsely ground black pepper
2 tsp chilli flakes
2 tsp freshly grated nutmeg
2 tsp ground cinnamon
2 tsp brown sugar
2 tsp dried thyme

Put all the ingredients in a glass jar and shake to mix well. Store in an airtight jar for up to 6 months.

Jerk BBQ sauce

Makes about 300g

We often get asked for a jerk BBQ sauce recipe from scratch, so here we have it for you guys – the perfect sweet sauce with a spicy jerk kick. You'll use this a lot, but can store it in the fridge for 3 months... more enjoyment!

250g tomato ketchup
1 tbsp jerk seasoning (see left)
1 tsp browning or 1 tbsp dark soy sauce
1 tsp apple cider vinegar
1 tsp salt
2 tbsp brown sugar
1 tbsp ground pimento (allspice)

Put the ketchup, jerk seasoning and browning in a pan, stir to combine, then bring to the boil over a medium heat. Add the remaining ingredients and bring back to the boil. Remove from the heat and leave to cool, then transfer to a sterilised jar and keep in the fridge.

Jerk-spiced lentil burger

Serves 4

A meaty, plump burger that every vegan craves once in a while. With the Jamaican jerk seasoning to bring that extra flava to it, you won't be able to tell it's a completely plant-based burger.

You can pan-fry the burger but we love it cooked on the BBQ grill – no more eating just the salad at the family BBQ, you'll be bossing them with pride, cooking this one up!

Add all the burger ingredients except the oil to a mixing bowl. Using your hands, combine the ingredients until uniform, squeezing lightly to mash the lentils; it should be a stodgy texture. Divide into 4 equal pieces and shape each into a ball, then flatten into burgers. Place on a plate, cover with kitchen paper and chill in the fridge for 1 hour, to firm up.

Heat a little oil in a frying pan over a medium-high heat until properly hot. Cook the burgers for 5–7 minutes on each side until browned and cooked through. If using cheese, place a slice on top of each 3 minutes before the end of cooking. Keep warm.

Add a likkle extra oil to the pan, dash in the sliced onion and cook over a high heat for 5 minutes until browned. Lightly toast the cut side of the buns in the same pan.

To assemble your burgers, spread mayo to the bottom half of the buns, then add the burger, followed by tomato, fried onions, BBQ sauce and lettuce. Top with the remaining half of the buns and nyam.

For the burgers

1 x 400g can green or brown lentils, drained
100g closed-cup mushrooms, diced
1½ tbsp jerk seasoning (see page 166 for homemade)
1 tsp dried thyme
1 tsp salt
1 tsp freshly ground black pepper
½ tsp ground pimento (allspice) or 5 crushed seeds
4 spring onions, finely chopped
150g porridge oats
1 tsp browning or 1 tbsp dark soy sauce
½ tbsp sugar
Juice of ½ lime
Vegetable oil, for frying

To serve

4 slices vegan cheese (optional)
½ medium onion, sliced
4 ciabatta burger buns, split in half
Vegan mayo
Jerk BBQ sauce (see page 166 for homemade)
Handful of lettuce leaves
1 large beef tomato, sliced

Jerk mushroom roti wraps

Serves 4

Portobello mushrooms cooked down in a jerk sauce, with colourful, sweet and crunchy vegetables, all wrapped in a Caribbean roti to create a perfect on-the-go lunch. The meatiness of the mushrooms is guaranteed to make you feel full.

Don't forget to drizzle some jerk BBQ sauce on it too! Or, if you prefer more heat, add some hot pepper or sweet chilli sauce!

In a mixing bowl, combine the slaw ingredients and place in the fridge until needed.

In a separate bowl, season the mushroom slices with the jerk paste, coating them all over. Heat a griddle pan over a medium-high heat until hot, then cook the mushrooms for 5 minutes, turning them until evenly cooked and a little charred.

Place the rotis or flatbreads on the work surface and add some slaw and jerk mushrooms, then a few slices of avocado and some BBQ sauce. Wrap up and nyam.

300g Portobello mushrooms, sliced 2cm thick
1 tbsp jerk paste
4 buss up shut rotis (see page 194) or shop-bought flatbreads
1 avocado, peeled, stoned and sliced
Jerk BBQ sauce (see page 166 for homemade), to serve

For the slaw
60g white cabbage, shredded
60g red cabbage, shredded
2 carrots, cut into julienne
½ onion, thinly sliced
150g drained canned sweetcorn
4 tbsp vegan mayo

Jerk BBQ cauliflower 'chicken wings'

Serves 4–6

Honestly the juiciest BBQ wings you could ever eat! And we've had quite a few in our lifetime... these are so, so juicy, and the BBQ sauce makes it oh-so finger-licking. Before creating these, we questioned whether these could ever work, and it turns out they do, incredibly well. If you grew up in South London, you know about Morley's BBQ chicken wings, but these are ten times better.

The jerk BBQ sauce and the coconut really do offer so much flavour! Indulge in these with some fries for your very own Friday night feast.

Preheat the oven to 180°C Fan/200°C/Gas 6.

Add the coconut milk to a mixing bowl with the salt, black pepper, pimento, thyme, garlic powder and chilli flakes or powder. Mix to combine, then add the cauliflower florets and mix to coat evenly.

Add the flour, cornflour and curry powder to a large plate and mix to combine.

Dip your spiced cauliflower florets (gently shaking off any excess liquid first) in the flour mixture to coat them all over then add them to a baking tray in a single layer. Bake in the oven for 40 minutes, turning them over halfway through cooking, until crispy.

Tip the crispy cauliflower into a clean mixing bowl, add the jerk BBQ sauce and mix together to coat. Tip back onto the tray in a single layer and place back in the oven for 10 minutes to caramelise.

Garnish with the spring onions and serve with vegan mayo.

200ml coconut milk
Pinch of salt
1 tsp freshly ground black pepper
1 tsp ground pimento (allspice)
1 tsp dried thyme
1 tsp garlic powder
1 tsp chilli flakes or powder
800g cauliflower (about 1 head),
    cut into florets
200g plain flour
1 tbsp cornflour
1 tsp curry powder
180g jerk BBQ sauce (see page 166
    for homemade)
2 spring onions, thinly sliced,
    to garnish
Vegan mayo, to serve

Meat-free kebabs

Kebabs are a British favourite takeaway that we had our fair share of growing up in South London, but the potential for a vegan version has always been there. There are some great plant-based kebabs out there that are a pretty similar to meat, so we've just added an extra spicy kick with our fiery scotch bonnet sauce.

Garlic mayo is another classic kebab shop condiment. If you can't find a vegan version in the shops you can make your own by mixing 2 crushed garlic cloves and a squeeze of lemon juice into 150g vegan mayo.

Heat enough oil in a frying pan for shallow-frying, then add the plantain and fry for 3–4 minutes until golden. Remove to a plate lined with kitchen paper, to absorb excess oil.

In a large mixing bowl, season the kebab pieces with salt and black pepper. Heat a likkle vegetable oil in a large frying pan over a medium heat and fry the kebab pieces until browned. Add the browning and scotch bonnet sauce to the pan, mix together and simmer for 10 minutes until the liquid has been absorbed. Remove from the heat.

Build your kebab by filling your roti, flatbread or pitta with some vegan garlic mayo, adding some scotch bonnet sauce to taste. Then add some lettuce, cabbage, onion, tomato, spring onion and fried plantain. Place some fried kebab pieces over everything and top off with more scotch bonnet sauce.

Vegetable oil, for frying
1 ripe plantain, peeled and sliced on the diagonal
350g meat-free kebab pieces
1 tsp browning or 1 tbsp dark soy sauce
4 tbsp scotch bonnet sauce (see page 215), plus extra to serve
4 buss up shut rotis (see page 194) or shop-bought flatbreads or pitta bread
2 tbsp vegan garlic mayo (see intro)
⅓ lettuce, shredded
⅓ red cabbage, shredded
1 onion, thinly sliced
1 large tomato, sliced
1 spring onion, thinly sliced
Salt and freshly ground black pepper

Jerk BBQ roast

Serves 6–8

We've created this seitan recipe, seasoned beautifully, for the perfect vegan Sunday dinner.

Preheat the oven to 180°C Fan/200°C/Gas 6.

Mix the wheat gluten, flour and jerk seasoning in a large mixing bowl. Combine the stock, wine, browning, maple syrup, hot pepper sauce and oil in a jug or bowl, then add to the dry ingredients, mix together and knead to form a dough. Mould into a beef joint shape (tying with string at intervals for the full authentic look) and place in a roasting tray. Throw the thyme, spring onions, garlic and scotch bonnet into the tray around the joint, and roast in the oven for 25 minutes.

Remove from the oven and brush the roast liberally with some of the jerk BBQ sauce, then place back in the oven and roast for a further 25 minutes.

For the gravy, add the remaining jerk BBQ sauce to a small pan with the water, stock granules and cornflour paste. Place over a medium heat and bring to a simmer, whisking, until you have a thick gravy.

Serve the roast with the gravy, a green veg such as beans and plantain mash (see page 92) or our rum-roasted potatoes (see page 207).

280g vital wheat gluten
100g plain flour
3 tbsp jerk seasoning (see page 166)
125ml vegan stock
250ml Red Label wine or red wine (ensure vegan)
1 tsp browning or 1 tbsp dark soy sauce
60ml maple syrup
2 tbsp hot pepper sauce
3 tbsp olive oil
Bunch of fresh thyme sprigs
6–8 spring onions, halved
6–8 garlic cloves, unpeeled
1 scotch bonnet pepper

For the gravy
300g jerk BBQ sauce (see page 166 for homemade)
250ml water
2 tbsp vegan stock granules
1 tsp cornflour mixed to a paste with a likkle water

Jerk tofu

We've seasoned up the tofu with dry jerk seasoning, and got a nice crisp coating on it by pan-frying it, then tossing it with some jerk BBQ sauce. It tastes unbelievable and is so quick to make – you'll love it. It's great served with bulgur wheat and peas (see page 204), fried plantain (see page 65) and avocado.

For the tofu, after draining off any water in the packet, place a plate on top of the blocks of tofu and press down on it for 30 seconds, then blot with kitchen paper to remove as much water as you can. Cut each block into 6 rectangular slabs, then place in a bowl, add the jerk seasoning to coat and set aside.

Heat the oil in a ridged griddle pan (or heavy frying pan) over a medium-high heat, add the tofu slices and use a smaller-sized pan to press on top of the tofu. Cook for 5 minutes on each side until crisp and golden, with good char lines if using a ridged pan. Place in a bowl, add the jerk BBQ sauce and stir gently to coat, then serve.

2 x 200g blocks of extra-firm tofu
4 tbsp jerk seasoning (see page 166)
2 tbsp olive oil
4 tbsp jerk BBQ sauce (see page 166 for homemade)

Fired Up Flava

Jerk BBQ veggies

Serves 4

There's no better feeling than lighting the BBQ on a hot summer day, and it really does enhance the flavours of food, taking them to exciting new heights. Like this recipe, simple everyday vegetables just need a likkle jerk seasoning and butter pon it, before grilling on the BBQ.

We've always said vegetables are the best ingredients to season, because – coupled with the incredible spices we like to use – the natural flavours that already come with veggies taste even better!

Get your BBQ hot. (Alternatively, you can grill the veggies in a ridged griddle pan on the hob, or under an oven grill.)

Put all the veggies in a mixing bowl, add the jerk seasoning, oil and melted butter and toss together.

Add the veggies individually to the BBQ and cook for 5–10 minutes on each side until char-grilled (or cook in a griddle pan or oven grill). Place on a large platter, ready to serve.

Mix the jerk BBQ sauce, water and stock granules in a small pan and warm over a medium heat to make a gravy.

Serve the grilled veggies with the gravy on the side.

1 red bell pepper, deseeded
    and quartered
1 yellow bell pepper, deseeded
    and quartered
2 Portobello mushrooms, halved
1 aubergine, quartered lengthways
1 courgette, quartered lengthways
4 spring onions, left whole
2 red onions, peeled and halved
2 tbsp jerk seasoning (see page 166)
2 tbsp olive oil
1 tbsp vegan butter, melted
4 tbsp jerk BBQ sauce
    (see page 166 for homemade)
250ml water
2 tsp vegan stock granules

Grilled chilli herb corn

Bring that extra flava to your BBQs with this wonderful sweet and spicy corn, infused with some of our favourite Caribbean spices, with a sweetness to bring some sunshine to your summer get-togethers.

Heat up your BBQ or ridged griddle pan.

Grab a mixing bowl and add the coconut oil, melted butter, garlic, pimento, scotch bonnet or chilli flakes, thyme, paprika, sugar, salt, black pepper, squeeze of lime and half the mint. Mix together well.

Brush most of the chilli herb mix over the corn cobs. Grill on the BBQ or in a griddle pan for about 10 minutes, turning every 2 minutes, until lightly charred all over.

Remove to a plate and brush with the remaining chilli-herb mix. Garnish with the parsley and remaining mint and serve with lime wedges. Time to nyam it up!

4 tbsp coconut oil
2 tbsp vegan better, melted
3 garlic cloves, very finely chopped
¼ tsp ground pimento (allspice)
  or 4 crushed pimento
  (allspice) berries
¾ scotch bonnet pepper, deseeded
  and diced, or 1 tbsp chilli flakes
1 tbsp dried thyme
1 tsp paprika
1 tbsp sugar
1 tsp salt
1 tsp freshly ground black pepper
Squeeze of lime juice, plus extra
  wedges to serve
Handful of mint leaves, chopped
4 corn on the cob
Handful of parsley leaves, chopped

Mango coleslaw

The perfect side for any dish! Life wouldn't be the same without slaw by your side: it's a very popular thing in the Caribbean community, and for us it was so important growing up. We've made this dish different by adding some mango for the sweetness and a kick of spice to complement. Perfect for BBQ parties with friends and family. Coleslaw is a must – trust us on this one!

In a large mixing bowl, add both cabbages, the carrots, mango, corn kernels, spring onions and coriander and toss to combine.

In a small bowl, mix the mayo, sweet chilli sauce and vinegar, with salt and black pepper to taste, and whisk until smooth. Add this to the vegetable bowl, mix together and serve.

½ white cabbage, shredded
¼ red cabbage, shredded
2 carrots, cut into julienne
1 mango, peeled, stoned and cut into julienne
1 corn on the cob, kernels sliced off
2 spring onions, thinly sliced
Handful of coriander leaves, finely chopped
230g vegan mayo
1 tbsp sweet chilli sauce
50ml apple cider vinegar
Salt and freshly ground black pepper

Sweet potato salad

Everybody needs a side dish on their plate, and this sweet potato salad is the perfect complement to any meal: sweet and spiced, and cooled with vegan mayo. A simple, easy dish for the family to enjoy. You can keep any leftovers in the fridge for a few days, to have with other meals.

Cook the sweet potatoes in boiling water until just tender, then drain and leave to cool completely.

Place in a mixing bowl, add the remaining ingredients with salt and black pepper to taste, and mix to combine.

300g sweet potatoes, peeled and cut into 2.5cm chunks
½ small red onion, finely diced
1 tbsp mixed dried herbs
1 green bell pepper, deseeded and diced
1 red bell pepper, deseeded and diced
75g drained canned sweetcorn
Handful of parsley leaves
4 tbsp vegan mayo
¼ scotch bonnet pepper, deseeded and diced
Salt and coarsely ground black pepper

Jerk BBQ fruit platter

Serves 6–8

Your BBQs have just got more exciting with this fruit platter! This recipe is sweet and spicy and so easy to make. What better way than taking the refreshing fragrant flavours of watermelon, pineapple, peaches, mango and plums with Jerk FLAVA! Perfect for family and friends in the summer.

Heat your BBQ or a griddle pan.

Place all the fruit in a large mixing bowl, add the jerk seasoning then toss together to coat.

In batches, place the fruit on the grill or griddle and cook for 2 minutes on each side, rotating it to create cross-hatch grill marks.

Place all the fruit on a large platter, garnish with mint leaves and dig in.

1 medium pineapple, peeled, cored, and cut into slices 1cm thick

4 plums, halved and stoned

4 peaches, halved and stoned

1 watermelon, peeled and cut into wedges 1–2cm thick

1 mango, peeled, stoned and sliced 1–2cm thick

2 tbsp jerk seasoning (see page 166)

Mint leaves, to garnish

LADS &
AUCES

Sides, Salads and Sauces   190

Warm and soft roti and fluffy rices for your curries, and fries for your burgers: we've got you covered with some absolutely flavalicious dishes in this chapter!

Sides are such an integral part to the food we grew up on, and we often paired two or more sides on our dinner plates. They were too good to turn away! We put our hearts and souls into our side dish creations, so we hope you'll absolutely love these recipes and turn to them for years to come.

The great thing about these is that you can mix and match; they're truly versatile. You'll find some delicious light and soulful sides and salads, creamy mac 'n' cheese, and some easy homemade sauces that will give your dishes that extra flava!

- "ITAL SIP" SOUP OF THE DAY — $800 J
- JAMAICAN GARDEN SALAD
SERVED WITH ITALIAN DRESSING & WHEAT TOAST. — $1000 J
- SIDE ORDERS
RASTA·PASTA· PLANTAIN W·FRITTER
FRIED PLANTAIN·ACKEE·CALLALOO
FRIES/RICE/BAMMY
TOFU· BEAN STEW — $600 J (EACH)
- NATURAL DESSERT
- FROZEN FRUIT WHIP
- FRESH FRUITS BASH — $800 J

(OUR FOOD IS PREPARED WITH COCONUT MILK &)
NATURAL SPICE

$
ML. 1,250 J
1,550 J
,200 J
200 J

Buss up shut rotis

Makes 4 large
or 6 smaller rotis

Buss up shut, aka paratha, is a popular type of roti in Trinidad and across some other parts of the Caribbean. It actually got the name from its resemblance to a torn T-shirt! Funny, eh?

It has a unique soft yet flaky texture and is incredibly delicious, especially with curries. It is usually cooked on a tawa – a massive, flat cast-iron pan – but you can easily use a frying pan or crêpe pan. The process is lengthy, but oh-so worth it. There are some photos on the next page to guide you.

Sift the flour into a large mixing bowl and add the baking powder, salt and sugar. Gradually add enough water to bring the mixture together, then knead into a soft, smooth dough. Rub oil over the dough, cover and set aside to rest for 30 minutes.

Once rested, divide the dough into 4 equal pieces or, if using a pan smaller than 30cm, into 6 pieces. Shape each piece into a ball, then press into a circle with your hands and roll out on a floured surface into a larger, thin circle, about 24cm in diameter (or the size of your tawa or frying pan), using a rolling pin. Rub softened butter onto the surface of each dough circle, and sprinkle a likkle flour over each.

Cut a slit from the middle of a dough circle to the edge, then roll from a cut edge around into a cone shape. Using your fingers, press and tuck what was the outside of the circle in towards the centre, to make more of a ball shape, then flip over and press the tip of the cone downwards into the dough, to complete the ball shape. Repeat with the rest of the dough circles, then cover the balls with a tea towel and leave to rest for 30 minutes–1 hour.

Heat your tawa or frying pan over a low-medium heat. Mix together the oil and melted butter for brushing and set aside.

Roll out your rested dough balls on a floured surface, first by pressing with your fingers to flatten, then by using a rolling pin to roll each into a large circle, about 24cm in diameter (or the size of your tawa or frying pan), flipping it and rolling on both sides. Make sure the edges are not thicker than the inside.

For the dough
500g plain flour, plus extra for dusting
4 tsp baking powder
1 tsp salt
2 tsp caster sugar
300–400ml water
1 tbsp vegetable oil
1 tbsp vegan butter, softened

For brushing
3 tbsp vegetable oil
3 tbsp vegan butter, melted

Once the pan is hot, pick up a dough circle and lay it on the hot pan, making sure it's flat. Be careful: it will be hot! Quickly brush with oil and melted butter on the surface of the roti, flip and repeat on the other side.

Move the roti around with a wooden spatula or spoon in a clockwise movement, and flip every 10 seconds, allowing the roti to cook evenly, until cooked through. You should start seeing slight brown cook marks. Then, using two wooden spoons or spatulas, clap the roti sides together from the edges towards the centre so they flake apart.

Remove from the pan, cover with a clean tea towel and rest for 15 minutes; this will make the roti softer and fluffier. Repeat with the remaining dough circles.

Sides, Salads and Sauces

195

Garlic hard-dough bread

Serves 6–8

We love a bit of innovation with the Caribbean foods we've grown up with, and there's no better one than this! Hard-dough bread is an absolute favourite for most people of Jamaican heritage. We've added an extra flava to it with the garlic as we felt the texture of hard-dough bread was just perfect for the job. It just made so much sense – and once you try this you will not regret it! Try it with our ackee and cabbage dish on page 28, in place of the dumplings, or with the spicy bolognese on page 75.

Preheat the oven to 200°C Fan/220°C/Gas 8.

Add the butter, garlic, parsley and salt to a mixing bowl, and mix di ting! Then cut the hard-dough loaf into thick slices, but not all the way through to the base. Spread the garlic butter onto both sides of each bread slice, making sure you get into the gaps. Then spread the top of the loaf with garlic butter.

Wrap the loaf in foil and bake in the oven for 30 minutes. Unwrap the loaf and continue cooking for a further 10–15 minutes until the sides are crisp. Remove from the oven and let it rest for 10 minutes, then BOOM! The ting done!

250g softened vegan butter or margarine
10 garlic cloves, finely chopped
15g parsley leaves, finely chopped
A likkle sea salt
1 large loaf of hard-dough bread (ensure vegan), unsliced

Mac 'n' cheese

Serves 6

Creamy, crunchy baked mac 'n' cheese, just how it should be made! A blend of spices to go alongside the creaminess makes this soul food heaven on a plate!

We love this extra special dish served with an array of our favourites, like bulgur wheat or rice and peas, a curry, plantain and some cooked-down veggies on the side. But, to be honest, we also just eat it on its own when we get that craving... and that's very often!

Preheat the oven to 160ºC Fan/180ºC/Gas 4.

Cook the pasta in a large pot of boiling, salted water according to the packet instructions, but taking a couple of minutes off the cooking time as it will cook further in the oven. Drain, return to the pan and stir in the butter to stop it sticking together.

Heat the oil in a separate pan, add the onion and cook for 3–5 minutes until just softened, then add the scotch bonnet and cook for another minute. Add the flour and cook, stirring, for a minute or two. Gradually add the milk, whisking to incorporate it after each addition. When all the milk is absorbed and you have a smooth sauce, simmer for 2–3 minutes, then add two-thirds of the cheese, the chilli powder, mustard, if using, and syrup. Mix together, add salt and pepper to taste, and simmer for a further 2–3 minutes.

Add the drained macaroni to the sauce and mix together, then tip into an ovenproof dish. Mix the remaining grated cheese with the breadcrumbs, sprinkle evenly over the top and bake in the oven for 30–35 minutes until golden brown and bubbling, with a crispy top.

500g dried spirali or macaroni pasta
1 tsp vegan butter
3 tbsp vegetable oil
1 medium onion, finely chopped
1 scotch bonnet pepper, deseeded and diced
2½ tbsp plain flour
500ml plant-based milk of your choice
300g vegan cheese, grated
1 tsp chilli powder
1 tsp English mustard (optional)
1 tsp golden syrup
75g breadcrumbs
Salt and freshly ground black pepper

Sides, Salads and Sauces

Ital pelau rice

Pelau is one of Trinidad's most iconic dishes and can be made in a variety of ways, usually using meat. Here we have used the traditional method but added our own natural flava to create an amazing Ital version that is just as good.

Heat the oil in a large pot over a high heat. Add the carrot, celery, onion, garlic, spring onions, bell peppers and tomato and cook down for 5 minutes, then add the green seasoning, salt, black pepper, sugar, ginger and thyme, mix together and cook for a few more minutes. Add the gungo peas and rice, crumble in the stock cubes, add the coconut milk and add enough water to cover the rice by 3cm. Stir to combine. Fling in the scotch bonnet, cover with a lid and cook over a low heat for 30 minutes until the rice is cooked.

Remove the scotch bonnet before serving.

2 tbsp vegetable oil
1 large carrot, diced
1 celery stick, diced
1 small onion, diced
2 garlic cloves, diced
2 spring onions, sliced
1 red bell pepper, deseeded
   and diced
1 green bell pepper, deseeded
   and diced
1 large tomato, chopped
1 tbsp green seasoning
   (see page 102)
½ tsp salt
½ tsp freshly ground black pepper
1 tbsp brown sugar
1 tsp grated fresh ginger
4 fresh thyme sprigs
1 x 400g can gungo peas, drained
   and rinsed
500g long-grain rice
2 vegan stock cubes
1 x 400ml can coconut milk
1 scotch bonnet pepper

Greens and beans

When FLAVA meets boring greens. When we have friends or family over we love the challenge of showing them new flavours on vegetables, and this dish is one of those!

Using softened vegetables from the Jamaican Rastafarian diet, we have added some texture to the dish by roasting seasoned butter beans.

Preheat the oven to 180°C Fan/200°C/Gas 6.

Line a baking tray with baking parchment. Add the butter beans in a single layer and season with the paprika, curry powder, thyme and salt and black pepper to taste. Drizzle over half the olive oil, mix around to coat the beans and roast in the oven for 15–20 minutes until crispy.

Meanwhile, bring a pot of water to the boil. Add a little salt, then the green beans, greens and tenderstem. Blanch for 2–3 minutes, then drain and set aside.

In a large pan, heat the vegetable oil, then add the garlic, scotch bonnet and ginger. Mix together for about 2 minutes, then add the tomato and cook down for a further 2 minutes. Add the drained beans, greens and tenderstem. Stir, adding the remaining olive oil and thoroughly mixing.

Finally, mix in the roasted butter beans. Top with chilli flakes or chilli oil, and serve.

1 x 400g can butter beans, drained and rinsed
1 tsp paprika
½ tsp curry powder
1 tsp dried thyme
2 tbsp olive oil
400g fine green beans
200g spring greens
300g tenderstem broccoli
2 tbsp vegetable oil
6 garlic cloves, diced
1 scotch bonnet pepper, deseeded and finely diced
Small knob of fresh ginger, peeled and grated
1 large tomato, diced
Salt and freshly ground black pepper
Chilli flakes or chilli oil, to serve

Bulgur wheat and peas

Serves 6–8

This version of the iconic Caribbean dish rice and peas has just as much flava but is much lighter. Bulgur wheat is packed with minerals, vitamins and fibre, and since balance is key to a great diet, this recipe is a perfect accompaniment to so many dishes and a great alternative to rice.

Add the kidney beans with their liquid to a saucepan, then add the coconut milk and browning, if using. Season with salt and black pepper to taste, then add the pimento, garlic, onion, spring onion, thyme sprigs and scotch bonnet. Bring to the boil, then turn down to a simmer and cook for 10 minutes.

Add the bulgur wheat, top up the water to cover the bulgur wheat by 3cm, if necessary, place a lid on the pan and cook over a low heat for 10–12 minutes until cooked and all the liquid is absorbed. Remove the scotch bonnet before serving.

1 x 400g can kidney beans, with their liquid
200ml coconut milk
¼ tsp browning or 1 tsp dark soy sauce (optional)
1 tsp pimento (allspice) berries
2 garlic cloves, finely chopped
1 small onion, finely chopped
1 spring onion, sliced
4–6 fresh thyme sprigs
1 scotch bonnet pepper
500g bulgur wheat
Salt and freshly ground black pepper

Special fried rice

Serves 4–6

An Asian and Caribbean fusion, where we swap eggs for ackee, which is similar in texture, but creamier, and an iconic flavour from Jamaica. Mixed with a lemongrass-infused chilli rice and soy sauce, it makes a delicious rice bowl dish to enjoy, and is a great way to use up leftover rice.

It's a really easy dish that sits perfectly on the dining table, and is sure to go down well with family and friends. Fragrant flavas, natural goodness, and comforting too.

Firstly, let's cook the rice. Rinse the rice well in a sieve, then add to a saucepan with enough water to cover it by 5cm. Bring to the boil, add the chilli flakes, garlic, lemongrass, butter and 1 teaspoon each of salt and black pepper. Stir, cover and simmer over a low heat until the rice is soft and fluffy. Remove from the heat.

Heat the sesame oil in a large frying pan over a medium heat. Add the onion, garlic, scotch bonnet and ginger and cook down for about 3 minutes until soft. Add the bell pepper, broccoli, mushrooms, carrot and spring onions, mix together, then add the thyme and pimento, season with salt and black pepper and cook for 5 minutes, or until the veg starts to soften.

Add in your cooked rice, then add the ackee and soy sauce and mix gently (nobody wants mushy ackee; treat it with TLC!). Fry for 5 minutes, then serve topped with spring onions and toasted coconut shavings.

The ting done!

2 tbsp sesame oil
1 onion, chopped
4 garlic cloves, chopped
½ scotch bonnet pepper, deseeded and finely chopped
Small knob of fresh ginger, peeled and grated
1 red bell pepper, deseeded and chopped
150g broccoli, diced
200g mushrooms, diced
1 large carrot, diced
2 spring onions, chopped, plus extra to garnish
1 tsp dried thyme
1 tsp ground pimento (allspice)
1 x 540g can ackee, drained
2 tbsp dark soy sauce
100g coconut shavings, toasted
Salt and freshly ground black pepper

For the rice
200g basmati rice
1 tsp chilli flakes
1 garlic clove, peeled
2 lemongrass stalks, bruised
1 tbsp vegan butter

Rum-roasted potatoes

Serves 4–6

Crunchy on the outside, melt-in-the-mouth creamy soft on the inside, these potatoes are infused with an unbelievable medley of flavas. We absolutely enjoy nyammin pon these golden treats.

You may be wondering how the rum works in this: we use dark rum when tossing the potatoes to get them all crumbly and to seep into the crispy parts when roasted.

The key to getting the right flava infusion into this dish is keeping the garlic skins on when roasting alongside the other vegetables – it bathes in the oil and infuses the potatoes to produce the most amazing taste.

Preheat the oven to 200°C Fan/220°C/Gas 7.

Bring a large pot of water to the boil, add your potatoes and a likkle salt. Par-boil for 10 minutes until beginning to soften slightly, then drain and toss them three or four times until rough around the edges. Add the rum, toss again to coat the potatoes, then add the salt, black pepper and paprika, and give them a final toss to distribute evenly.

Heat the butter and olive oil in a large roasting tin in the preheated oven, then when the butter is melted and the oil is hot, add the garlic, pimento, herb sprigs and scotch bonnet, then add the potatoes, spreading them out so they have at least 1cm of space between them. Roast for 40–45 minutes, turning them over halfway through and adding the spring onions about 5 minutes before the end of the roasting time, until the potatoes are crispy and golden.

1kg potatoes (Maris piper or baking potatoes are best), peeled and quartered (or cut into 6 or 8 if very large)
50ml dark or spiced rum
½ tsp salt
¼ tsp coarsely ground black pepper
1 tsp paprika
75g unsalted vegan butter
4 tbsp olive oil
4 garlic cloves, unpeeled
4–6 pimento (allspice) berries or ¼ tsp ground
3–4 fresh rosemary or thyme sprigs
1 scotch bonnet pepper
2 spring onions, chopped
Salt and coarsely ground black pepper

Yam fries with scotch bonnet sauce or chilli jam

Serves 6–8

Yam is a great, versatile starchy veg, similar to potato, but with way more depth, so it makes a fantastic alternative when making fries. Switch up your fries a likkle with this crunchy side piece.

Peel your yam, then slice it into chip shapes, making them as evenly sized as possible. Bring a pan of water to the boil, add the yam and par-boil for 5–7 minutes. Drain, then pat dry with kitchen paper and place in a mixing bowl. Season da ting with salt and black pepper and the thyme, then add the cornflour and mix together well, making sure the yam is evenly coated.

Half-fill a large, deep, heavy pan with vegetable oil and place over a high heat. Heat to 160°C – to test if the oil is hot enough, drop in a piece of bread; if it turns golden in 30 seconds, it's ready. Fry the yam chips in batches for 3–4 minutes until golden brown. Remove with a slotted spoon to a plate lined with kitchen paper, to drain excess oil, and serve with the scotch bonnet sauce or chilli jam.

600g white or yellow yam
1 tsp dried thyme
1 tbsp cornflour
Vegetable oil, for deep-frying
Salt and freshly ground black pepper
Scotch bonnet sauce or chilli jam
   (see page 215), to serve

Sides, Salads and Sauces

209

Roasted butternut and chickpea salad with coconut mint dressing

Serves 4

A delicious wholesome salad, with crunch, spices and sweetness; sometimes you just need that salad to bring balance to your diet, and this one is perfect for the job. The butternut squash and spiced chickpeas provide that added flava to make you fuller for longer too! And the coconut mint sauce makes it extra satisfying.

Preheat the oven to 180°C Fan/200°C/Gas 6.

Put the squash in a big mixing bowl with the chickpeas and season with the paprika and salt and black pepper to taste. Add the syrup and a drizzle of olive oil, then mix to coat. Spread the squash out in a single layer on a large roasting tray. Spread the chickpeas out on a separate tray. Roast the squash for 30–35 minutes until cooked and caramelised, turning the pieces halfway through, and the chickpeas for 20 minutes. Remove and leave to cool.

Meanwhile, for the chopped salad, put the bell pepper and sweetcorn in a mixing bowl with the lettuce. Season with a likkle salt and pepper and drizzle with olive oil. Toss and mix together, cover and leave in the fridge until ready to serve.

Make the dressing by mixing the yoghurt, syrup and mint together in a small bowl.

In a large serving dish, combine the chopped salad with the cooled roasted squash and chickpeas. Spoon over the dressing and serve.

300g butternut squash, peeled, deseeded and cut into chunks and/or crescents
1 x 400g can chickpeas, drained and rinsed
2 tbsp paprika
2 tbsp golden syrup
Olive oil, for drizzling
1 red bell pepper, deseeded and cut into chunks
1 x 198g can sweetcorn, drained and rinsed
1 romaine lettuce, leaves separated and chopped
Salt and freshly ground black pepper

For the dressing
250g coconut yoghurt
2 tbsp golden syrup
15g fresh mint leaves, finely chopped

Ital fruit salad

Serves 4

A beautiful, sweet salad full of tropical fruits and coated in a sticky dressing. We love the mixture of vibrant fruit and crunchy vegetables in our salads – it just adds extra excitement to the dish. Serve as a side on a brunch/lunch/dinner table, or eat by itself on a sunny day. Give it a go, we're sure you'll love it.

To make your dressing, add the guava jam, vinegar and a likkle water to a small saucepan. Cook down over a medium heat for 5 minutes until smooth, then remove from the heat and leave to cool.

Put your prepared fruit and veg in a large bowl with the herbs, and mix together.

Pour the cooled dressing over the salad, toss to mix, then serve.

1 papaya, peeled, deseeded
  and sliced
2 passionfruit, halved
400g fresh peeled pineapple,
  cut into chunks
2 kiwi fruit, peeled and sliced
1 red cos lettuce, leaves separated
½ cucumber, halved lengthways
  and sliced
¼ white cabbage, shredded
¼ red cabbage, shredded
Handful of parsley leaves
Handful of basil leaves

For the dressing
4 tbsp guava jam
2 tsp apple cider vinegar

Chilli bean and avocado salad

Serves 6–8

A crunchy salad is always needed at a dinner table, and this one is a real easy go-to when you're looking for just that. Packed with nutritious ingredients that complement every and any meal.

No boring salads round here. Just great textures, and nuff flavas!

1 x 400g can mixed beans, drained and rinsed
2 large avocados, peeled, stoned and chopped
1 large tomato, diced
100g raw sweetcorn kernels (sliced off 1 fresh cob)
⅓ red cabbage, finely shredded
⅓ white cabbage, finely shredded
3 spring onions, finely chopped
1 red bell pepper, deseeded
  and diced
1 green bell pepper, deseeded
  and diced
1 tsp chilli flakes
2 tbsp lime juice
2 tbsp extra virgin olive oil
Salt and freshly ground black pepper

Add all the ingredients, with salt and pepper to taste, to a large mixing bowl. Toss together and serve.

Chilli jam

Makes about 3 jars

Ohhh yes this is one of our favourite go-to condiments. It's so versatile – serve with fried plantain, fries and yam fries (see page 208), or as a dip or marinade, or fling some in a stew for the perfect sweet and spicy balance!

10 red scotch bonnet peppers, deseeded
4 garlic cloves, peeled
2–3 red bell peppers, deseeded and roughly chopped
900g jam sugar
500ml apple cider vinegar
2 red chillies
Salt

Add the scotch bonnets, garlic and bell peppers to a blender or food processor. Pulse for 30 seconds, until smooth.

Transfer to a saucepan over a medium heat and add the sugar and vinegar. Bring to the boil, stirring. Pierce the red chillies with a knife, add to the pan and boil for 10–15 minutes until thick and smooth, stirring occasionally. Remove from the heat and leave to cool for 10 minutes, then add salt to taste and transfer to warm, sterilised jars.

Seal and leave to set for a few hours. Once opened, store in the fridge.

Scotch bonnet sauce

Makes 1 jar

If you want that extra bit of spice, zing, pow in your food, then this right here is the one! Feel the fire and test your heat tolerance with our pepper sauce. All you'll need are a few simple ingredients and a blender and saucepan, and a jar to store it in the fridge!

10 red scotch bonnet peppers, deseeded
1 red bell pepper, deseeded and roughly chopped
1 large tomato, quartered
2 spring onions, chopped
50ml apple cider vinegar
2 tbsp brown sugar
1 tsp ground pimento (allspice)
2 tsp salt

Add the scotch bonnets, bell pepper, tomato and spring onions to a blender and pulse for 2–3 minutes.

In a medium saucepan, bring the vinegar, sugar, pimento and salt to a simmer, stirring to dissolve the sugar. Add the blended ingredients to the saucepan and return to a simmer. Cook for 2–3 minutes, then remove from the heat and leave to cool slightly. Store in a sterilised jar in the fridge.

Mango chilli sauce

Makes 1 jar

For those who like a sweet, fruity and spicy kick in their dishes.

1 ripe mango, peeled and stoned
10 scotch bonnet peppers, deseeded
1 yellow bell pepper, deseeded and roughly chopped
4 garlic cloves, peeled
Leaves from 4–6 fresh thyme sprigs
50ml apple cider vinegar

Add all the ingredients to a blender pulse for 2–3 minutes until blended. Transfer it to a saucepan, bring to the boil, then simmer for 10 minutes, stirring. Remove from the heat and leave to cool slightly. Store in a sterilised jar in the fridge for up to 3 weeks.

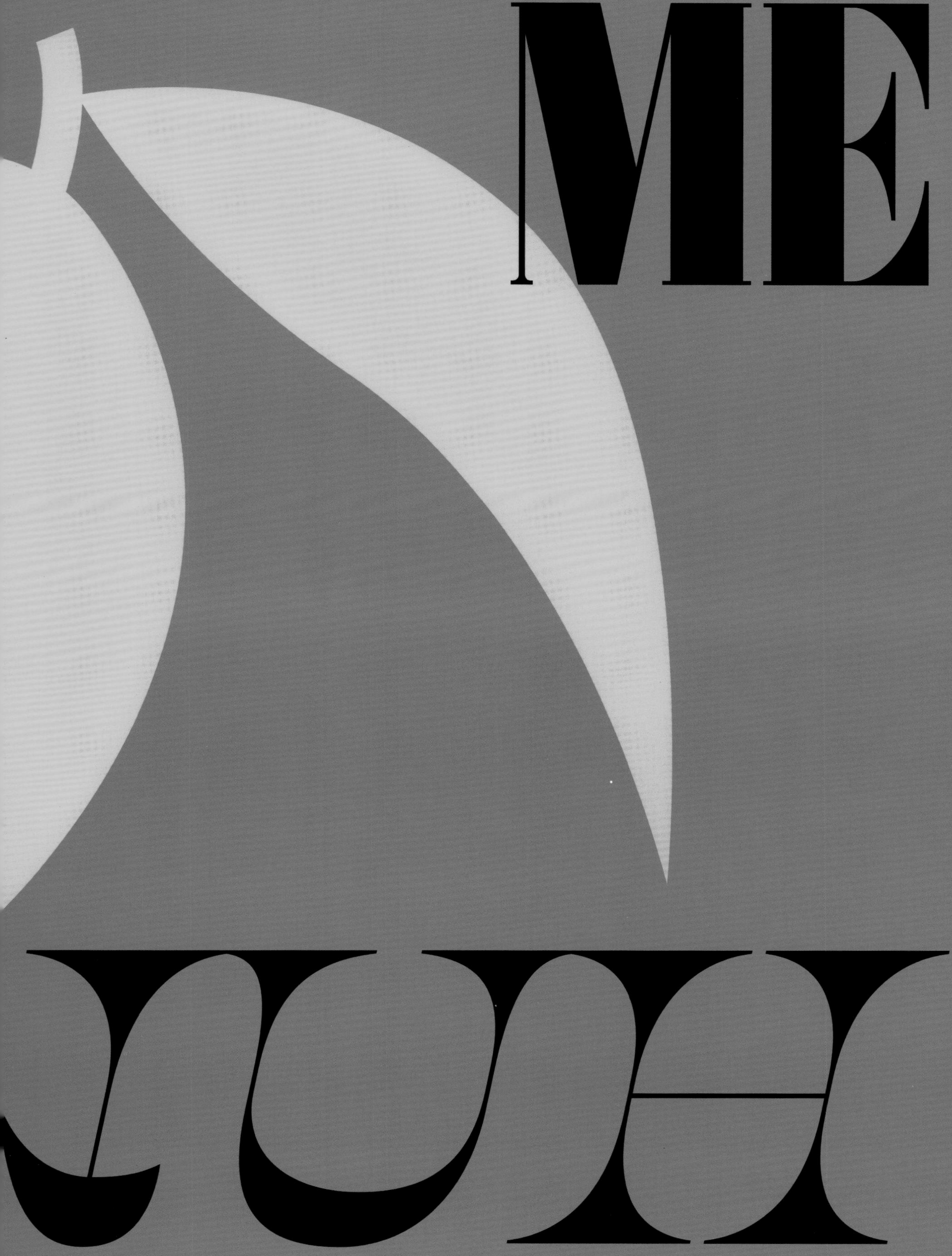
ME

Sweet Me Nuh   218

There's nothing like a sweet treat to just make you feel good! There's a taboo about vegan treats being bland and boring – bwoi, they never seen our recipes! This chapter is all about incredible indulgent flavours that will melt in your mouth and make you crave more and more (in moderation, of course!).

Inspired by our Caribbean upbringing, the recipes are filled with lots of sweet spices and punchy flavours, and include plantain choc chip cookies, yam and sweet potato chocolate pudding cake and vegan remixes of our sweet Caribbean favourites like carrot juice, ginger cake, and loads more.

We named this chapter 'sweet me nuh' which is a Jamaican patois saying that translates to something like, 'Do me a favour' or, 'Do it just for me!' Everyone can relate to a desire for a sweet treat at 3pm or on the weekend, and these recipes will bring that added joy to those cheeky times!

Sweet Me Nuh

Plantain and apple crumble

Serves 4–6

Crumble has to be one of our favourite desserts, so we've added in one of our favourite plant-based ingredients: plantain. Plantain honestly makes everything a hundred times better, and it's no different in this heavenly crumble. Chunks of it with apples, caramelised in a buttery spiced mixture... we just can't get enough of this crumble, and nor will you.

The riper the plantain, the sweeter the crumble will taste. To make your plantains overripe, just pop them in the oven at 180°C Fan/200°C/Gas 6 for about 15 minutes.

Serve with vegan vanilla ice cream, or custard.

Preheat the oven to 180°C Fan/200°C/Gas 6.

First, make the crumble. In a mixing bowl, combine the flour and sugar. Add the butter and rub it into the dry ingredients with your fingertips until you have a crumbly, even mixture. Set aside.

For the filling, melt the butter in a large pan over a low-medium heat, add the apples and toss around to cook for 2–3 minutes, then add the plantain, stir and cook for 2–3 minutes until the edges of the fruit begin to get a bit of colour and soften. Add the vanilla, cinnamon, nutmeg, bay leaf and salt, and stir to combine. Finally, add 200ml apple juice, stir everything together and simmer for 1–2 minutes.

Tip the apple and plantain mixture into a large ovenproof dish, about 23cm square, and remove the bay leaf. Add the rest of the apple juice to the mixture, sprinkle the crumble evenly on top and bake in the oven for 35–40 minutes until the crumble is cooked and golden brown.

1 tbsp vegan butter
3 apples, cored and cut
    into 2cm chunks
3 ripe plantain, peeled
    and cut into 2cm chunks
1 tbsp vanilla extract
1 tsp ground cinnamon
½ tsp freshly grated nutmeg
1 bay leaf
A likkle salt
300ml apple juice

For the crumble
225g plain flour
125g soft light brown sugar
125g vegan butter, cubed

Plantain choc chip cookies

Makes 6–8

These are one of those treats you'll find yourself indulging in without knowing how many you've actually eaten! A delicious home comfort, reminds us of times where we sat down with Nan for a chat over tea and biscuits – it brings back so many happy memories.

The sweet plantain marries with the mature cocoa chocolate, which melts into the cookies perfectly.

In a large mixing bowl, add both sugars, the salt and butter and cream together with a wooden spoon until smooth and combined. Add the vanilla and mix again.

Sift in the flour and baking powder and mix until smooth. Fold in the chocolate bar chunks and mashed plantain. Bring together into a fat disc, cover with cling film and place in the fridge for 30 minutes to set.

Preheat the oven to 180ºC Fan/200ºC/Gas 6 and line a large baking tray with baking parchment.

Spoon 6–8 portions of the dough onto the lined baking tray, spacing them well apart as they will spread (you might need 2 baking trays). Bake for 15 minutes until golden brown and cooked.

Leave to cool on the tray, then store in an airtight container for up to 2 days.

75g caster sugar
75g brown sugar
½ tsp salt
100g vegan butter or margarine
½ tsp vanilla extract
200g plain flour
1 tsp baking powder
150g vegan cocoa bar, broken into pieces
1 overripe plantain, peeled and mashed

Plantain bread

A warming, moist and sweet bread that is definitely something you look forward to making on a weekend. Growing up in a Caribbean household, these types of bread/cakes were always around – it was a comforting treat to look forward to having while watching a film or chilling with the fam. We love to eat it with a bowl of warm, creamy custard or as a cheeky treat on a Monday afternoon.

Preheat the oven to 160°C Fan/180°C/Gas 4. Grease a 900g/2lb loaf tin and line with baking parchment.

In a bowl and using a wooden spoon, mix together the butter and sugar until light and fluffy. (Feel free to use an electric mixer if you have one.)

Add in the apple sauce, yoghurt, flour, baking powder, cinnamon, salt, vanilla and raisins, if using. Add the mashed plantain and stir in until fully combined.

Spoon the mixture into the prepared tin and spread it out evenly. Give it a likkle shake, then bake in the oven for about 60–75 minutes until golden brown.

Leave to cool in the tin for about 15 minutes, then remove it from the tin, slice and enjoy!

200g vegan butter, plus extra for greasing
130g brown sugar
2 tbsp apple sauce
2 heaped tbsp coconut yoghurt
300g plain flour
1½ tsp baking powder
1 tsp ground cinnamon
½ tsp salt
2 tsp vanilla extract
60g raisins (optional)
4 overripe plantain, peeled and mashed

Christmas is all about rum cake in the Caribbean community, and without it you'd be pretty upset… so we've made a vegan version! And we think the taste is better than the dairy version.

It is similar to British Christmas pudding, but with a Caribbean twist – soaked dried fruit in wine, spices and a whole lot of rum! The soaking process is somewhat sacred, and some soak their fruit for a whole year, which makes the flavour even more intense.

We love to eat this with vegan custard, ice cream or just on its own.

Soak the dried fruit and glacé cherries in all the wine and half the rum overnight, or for as long as you can.

Preheat the oven to 160°C Fan/180°C/Gas 4.

Grease two 23cm round cake tins and line with baking parchment.

Tip the soaked fruit mixture into a blender or food processor and blend until almost smooth.

In a medium bowl, cream the butter and sugar together until smooth and fluffy (use electric beaters if you have them).

Combine the flour, baking powder, spices and salt in a large bowl. Add the flaxseed, vanilla, browning and creamed butter and sugar, then the blended fruit, and mix to combine (again, using electric beaters if you have them). The batter should be thick but pourable.

Divide the batter between the 2 prepared cake tins and bake in the middle of the oven for 1 hour until a toothpick inserted into the centre comes out clean. Keep an eye on them while they are baking; if they start to colour too quickly, cover loosely with foil.

Leave to cool in the tins, then drizzle over the remaining rum. Once removed from the tins, decorate with some glacé cherries.

- 500g mixed dried fruit (raisins, orange peel, currants, etc)
- 200g glacé cherries, plus extra to decorate
- 250ml Red Label wine or red wine (ensure vegan)
- 350ml white rum
- 115g unsalted vegan butter, plus extra for greasing
- 200g brown sugar
- 500g plain flour
- 1 tsp baking powder
- ½ tsp ground mixed spice
- ½ tsp ground cinnamon
- ½ tsp ground cloves
- ½ tsp freshly grated nutmeg
- ½ tsp ground ginger
- 1 tsp salt
- 1 tbsp ground flaxseed, soaked in 1 tbsp water
- 1 tsp vanilla extract
- 90ml browning

Sticky ginger cake

A warm and comforting cake that makes you go hmmm. One of Craig's favourites, and a traditional Caribbean favourite too, we've brought the vegan touch to this one, with the ginger really igniting the flavours. It's one of those dessert dishes that you have with a bit of custard or ice cream, kick your feet up and watch a good film. You might fall asleep, though... you've been warned!

Preheat the oven to 160ºC Fan/180ºC/Gas 4. Grease a 23cm round cake tin and line with baking parchment.

Add the butter, sugar, golden syrup, molasses, almond milk and apple sauce to a small pan and place over a low heat until melted and nicely combined. Set aside to cool.

Add the flour, bicarb, ginger, cinnamon, nutmeg and salt to a bowl and mix together. Add the melted ingredients and fold together.

Pour the mixture into the prepared tin and give it a likkle shake so it spreads out evenly.

Bake for 35–40 minutes until cooked through and a toothpick inserted into the centre comes out clean. Brush with syrup to glaze, and let cool before slicing.

175g vegan butter or margarine, softened, plus extra for greasing
100g dark brown sugar
100g golden syrup, plus an extra 2–3 tbsp to glaze
200ml molasses
200ml almond milk
250g apple sauce
300g self-raising flour
1 tsp bicarbonate of soda
2 tbsp ground ginger
2 tsp ground cinnamon
1 tsp freshly grated nutmeg
A likkle salt

Sweet Me Nuh

Sweet Me Nuh

Yam and sweet potato chocolate pudding cake

Serves 6–8

This sweet treat is a fusion of a thick, traditional Caribbean sweet potato pudding and a rich chocolate cake. Because of its dense consistency, we decided to call it a pudding cake – it is sooo comforting eaten warm, with that special melt-in-your-mouth feel.

We had to really pull ourselves away from this one, as we kept going back to taste some more! The sweet potato and yams make the texture silky smooth, and enhance the dark chocolate flavours to make it more satisfying.

If you don't have access to yam, just use extra sweet potato instead.

Preheat the oven to 180°C Fan/200°C/Gas 6 and line a 23cm round cake tin with baking parchment.

Cook the yam and sweet potato separately in boiling water until tender, then drain. For the topping, add a quarter of each to a food processor (while still hot), reserving the remaining for the cake. Add the chocolate, sugar and almond milk and process until the chocolate has melted, and it's all nice and smooth. Check the sweetness, adding more sugar if needed. Set aside.

Now for the cake. Place the reserved yam and sweet potato in a mixing bowl, add the almond milk, melted butter, chocolate, sugar, vanilla and browning and stir well to combine. In a separate bowl, combine the flour, cocoa powder, baking powder, salt and nutmeg. Sift into the wet ingredients and fold together until you have a thick batter.

Pour the mixture into the prepared tin and bake in the oven for 40–45 minutes, or until a toothpick inserted in the middle comes out clean.

Remove from the oven and leave to cool completely before spreading over the topping, using a palette knife. Alternatively, serve it warm as a pudding, with the topping on the side.

300g peeled white or yellow yam, cut into chunks
300g peeled sweet potato, cut into chunks

For the chocolate topping
60g dark chocolate (70% cocoa solids), roughly chopped
3 tbsp sugar
150ml almond milk

For the cake mixture
350ml almond milk
200g vegan butter, melted
150g dark chocolate (70% cocoa solids), chopped
300g brown sugar
1 tsp vanilla extract
1 tsp browning
350g plain flour
80g cocoa powder
1 tsp baking powder
1 tsp salt
¼ tsp freshly grated nutmeg

Sweet Me Nuh

Spice bun is a must-have in every Caribbean household over Easter and was an absolute staple for us growing up. But the queues stretching round the corner at our local Caribbean bakery made us create our own recipe. With Mum being vegan, we've adjusted it for her, and it tastes the same! Sweet and spiced and everything nice!

This is usually served with a slice of cheese between two slices of bun, like a sandwich, or eaten by itself, or spread with a bit of butter. Its versatility makes this all the better!

Preheat the oven to 160°C Fan/180°C/Gas 4. Grease a 450g/1lb loaf tin and line with baking parchment.

In a bowl, mix together the flour, baking powder, salt and spices and set aside.

Melt the butter in a large pan over a high heat, then add the wine, Guinness, sugar and vanilla. Stir until the sugar has dissolved and the alcohol has evaporated, then remove from the heat and set aside to cool completely. Once cool, stir in the flaxseed mixture.

Tip half the flour mixture into the liquid pan, with half the dried fruits and cherries, and fold to combine. Tip in the remaining flour mixture, dried fruit and cherries and fold again. Add the jam and browning then mix to a thick but sloppy consistency.

Tip the mixture into the prepared tin and bake in the centre of the oven for 1 hour, or until a toothpick inserted into the middle comes out clean.

Remove from the oven and leave to cool in the tin for 1 hour, before brushing over the syrup to glaze. Remove from the tin, slice and serve with cheese.

325g plain flour
1 tbsp baking powder
Pinch of salt
1 tsp each ground cinnamon, ground mixed spice and freshly grated nutmeg
60g vegan butter, plus extra for greasing
100ml Red Label wine or red wine (ensure vegan)
1 x 284ml bottle of Guinness or Dragon Stout
160g soft dark brown sugar
1 tsp vanilla extract
1 tbsp ground flaxseed mixed with 20ml water
150g dried mixed fruit (raisins, mixed peel, currants, etc)
100g glacé cherries
1 tbsp guava or strawberry jam
½ tsp browning
2 tbsp golden syrup
Sliced vegan cheese, to serve

Soursop juice

A thick, creamy and refreshing drink that is loved in Jamaica, and by us too. We used to really enjoy getting a bottle of this from our local Caribbean shop, and now we're showing you the secret recipe! If you're in the Brixton area or near vegetable stands that sell Caribbean produce, they should have this special fruit there too.

Soursop is quite large and unique looking, with a thick, stringy pulp texture inside, and it's one of the sweetest fruits there is.

Peel the soursop and remove the seeds. Put the fruit in a blender, add the water and blend until smooth.

Place a sieve over a large bowl or jug and line the sieve with a piece of cheesecloth or muslin. Strain the blended mixture through the sieve, pressing down on the pulp to extract as much liquid as possible, then stir in the condensed milk, almond milk, vanilla, lime juice and nutmeg, and mix.

Add sugar to taste and serve.

1 soursop
1 litre water
4 tbsp sweetened condensed coconut milk or vegan condensed milk
125ml almond milk
1 tbsp vanilla extract
Juice of 1 lime
Grating of fresh nutmeg
Sugar, to taste

Sorrel punch

Serves 6–8

The holiday season in the Caribbean is all about music, family, food, drinks and fun. Yes, in that order, lol. When we were younger we looked forward to a chilled glass of sorrel, made from hibiscus plant, which we usually had growing outside.

Living in London means that sourcing fresh sorrel is almost impossible, so we resort to buying the dried version, which is also good. We've put a likkle rum punch spin on this recipe to get you in the party spirit, yeahhhh mon! It's very versatile too – you can heat it and enjoy it as a hot drink but, for sure, however you drink it you'll love it!

Add the sorrel to a pot then add the water, ginger and citrus peels. Leave to soak overnight.

The next day, bring to the boil then add the sugar and stir well to dissolve. Add the orange and pineapple juice, cinnamon, grated nutmeg, cloves, wine and rum, then allow to warm through for 20 minutes over a very low heat, without simmering.

Let it cool for 10 minutes before straining into a large jug to serve, with ice and orange slices.

150g dried sorrel
1 litre water
1 tbsp grated fresh ginger
Peel of 1 orange
Peel of 1 lemon
Peel of 1 lime
4 tbsp caster sugar, or to taste
250ml orange juice
250ml pineapple juice
1 cinnamon stick
1 whole nutmeg, freshly grated
4–6 cloves
½ bottle Red Label wine or red wine (ensure vegan)
50ml white rum
Orange half slices and ice, to serve

Carrot juice

Serves 4

People often think this is a detox drink, but it's more of an indulgent milkshake. As it's one of our favourite Caribbean drink treats, we had to make a vegan version of it! Our nan taught us how to make it when we were growing up, and we often have it for special occasions like Christmas and Easter. It's also often drunk after dinner, or during the day in front of the TV. Craig used to place special orders with Nan for it whenever he got the carrot juice urge.

We know lots of Caribbeans love it too, and often ask us for a vegan version, so here it is in all its creamy glory! If you're feeling a bit cheeky, dash in a likkle rum, just like Nan does. It always makes things taste even better.

Place the carrots in a blender or food processor, add the water and blend until smooth.

Pour the mixture through a sieve into a jug or bowl. Use a spoon to press down on the carrot pulp to get as much juice out as you can. Discard the pulp.

Stir the liquid in the jug or bowl, then add the coconut milk, cinnamon, nutmeg, vanilla and rum, if using. Serve over ice.

500g carrots, peeled, and cut into chunks
1 litre water
1 x 400ml can coconut milk
1 tsp ground cinnamon
1 tsp freshly grated nutmeg
1 tsp vanilla extract
100ml white rum (optional)
Handful of ice, to serve

Guinness punch

Serves 4

A staple, comforting beverage in the Jamaican household – it's tradition to have this drink on a Sunday or at festive times. Basically, whenever you see this creamy beige liquid in a large jug on the table, you know it's a special occasion!

A combination of sweetness, spice and the bitter punch of Guinness makes this one of our favourite drinks ever – especially this vegan version!

Put everything in a blender and blitz! Serve over ice.

3 x 440ml cans Guinness
1 large handful of ice
1 x 320g can sweetened
  condensed coconut milk
  or vegan condensed milk
150ml plant-based milk
  of your choice
1 tsp freshly grated nutmeg
1 tsp ground cinnamon
1 tsp vanilla extract
A likkle rum (optional)

Irish moss

Serves 4

Irish moss is a traditional Caribbean drink, nicknamed 'strong back' for its fortifying qualities. It is very rich, and packed full of vitamins, nutrients and flava. We have created a fully plant-based version that is much healthier and lighter than that traditional one. Sea moss is the key ingredient to this recipe, and you should be able to find it in health food shops.

2 tbsp sea moss gel (see right)
2 tbsp ground flaxseed, soaked
   in 50ml water
1 x 400ml can coconut milk,
   or 400ml oat milk
1 x 320g can sweetened
   condensed coconut milk
   or vegan condensed milk
½ tsp freshly grated nutmeg
½ tsp ground mixed spice
½ tsp ground cinnamon
1 tsp vanilla extract
330ml Guinness or stout
25ml white rum (optional)

Add the sea moss gel to a blender with the soaked flaxseed and coconut milk, then blend to combine.

Stir in the condensed milk, spices, vanilla, Guinness, and rum, if using, and pour over ice to serve.

Sea moss gel

Makes 500ml

50g dried sea moss
1 litre tap water
Juice of 1 lemon
Juice of 1 lime
50ml spring water

Wash the sea moss thoroughly in water to remove any dirt and debris, then add to a large bowl with the tap water, lemon and lime juice and soak for 12–24 hours.

After soaking, the sea moss should have expanded. Give it a rinse then add to a blender with the spring water. Blend until smooth and creamy, like a gel.

Store in a clean jar in the fridge for up to 1 month, or freeze in ice-cube trays for up to 3 months.

Ingredients

ACKEE
One of the most-loved ingredients from Jamaica, and the most delicious too. As a fruit from the ackee tree, it's highly sought after and an integral part of Ital cooking. It's easily accessible in UK supermarkets these days and well worth its premium value. Cooked in minutes from the can, it has a deliciously soft texture, similar to eggs, and is often cooked down with onions and peppers.

ALL-PURPOSE SEASONING
A mixture of essential powdered spices including black pepper, pimento and garlic used to enhance dishes. Every Caribbean has this in their cupboard and you need it too, to get that EXTRA FLAVA!

AVOCADO
Also known as 'pear' in Jamaica, often sliced, and used as a side to a dish. The oils in the fruit are also beneficial in natural hair formulas.

BANANA BLOSSOM
Currently a new trend on the vegan scene with a similar texture to jackfruit. It fries beautifully as the edges go extra crunchy, while the insides stay soft. It is a great source of nutrients, and is particularly high in potassium.

BANANAS
Green bananas are a staple in Caribbean cooking and used as a simple side alongside dumplings with a stew, curry or cooked-down ackee.

BAY LEAF
A long-lasting and powerfully fragrant leaf used whole to bring a unique aroma to rice dishes, soups, curries and stews.

BEANS AND PEAS
Kidney beans, pigeon or black-eyed peas are often used interchangably in multiple dishes, for example, any of these beans could be used when making rice and peas. They are frequently used in soups and stews and are essential to have in your cupboard.

BREADFRUIT
Similar to potato in taste, high in fibre and incredibly versatile to cook with: it can be fried, grilled or roasted.

BROWNING
Made of caramelised sugar, it is added to stews and vegetables and some cakes to give a rich brown colour to dishes.

CALLALOO
A leafy vegetable similar to spinach, which can be used as an alternative. Tinned callaloo is available in supermarkets.

CAULIFLOWER
A succulent vegetable that soaks up flavour very well. Because of the rough edges it holds lots of sauce and batter, making it the perfect comfort food when roasted or fried.

COCONUT
The green ones, known as young coconuts, can be cut open to reveal lots of thirst-quenching coconut water inside to drink and jellied flesh to eat. The older, brown coconuts are more recognisable in the UK and contain less juice and drier flesh.

COCONUT CONDENSED MILK
Brings a thickness to our sweet beverages, and the coconut element adds an exotic touch.

COCONUT MILK
An integral part of rice and peas and many curries. It adds a delicious creaminess to a dish.

COCONUT OIL
A good option for cooking. It comes in solid form but liquidises quickly in the pan or in hot weather.

CORIANDER
Also known as cilantro in some parts of the world, this herb brings a zing to your meals. Used often in Trinidadian sauces and curries.

CORNMEAL
Ground to fine, medium and coarse consistencies. We use it in cornmeal porridge, but also in cakes, puddings and dumplings.

CURRY POWDER
A blend of aromatic spices to make the perfect Jamaican curry: ground turmeric, chilli powder, coriander, cumin and more. It's a great way to add some colour to your dishes too!

FLAXSEED
Often used as an egg replacement in cakes; when mixed with water it creates a gel that helps bind the mixture together.

FRUIT
Fruit is an integral part of the Caribbean diet, and we often use it to brighten up our dishes and drinks too. Mango, pawpaw (papaya), passionfruit, guava, soursop, sweetsop (custard apple) and many others.

GINGER
The taste and health benefits ginger brings to dishes make it a popular ingredient in many Ital dishes.

GREEN SEASONING
A wet, herby mixture used as a seasoning in many different Caribbean dishes. It is a blend of coriander, parsley, garlic, ginger, spring onions and more.

HARD FOOD
The name for staple starchy foods, such as boiled dumplings, yam, green bananas, usually eaten alongside a main meal. It's also known as provisions.

JACKFRUIT
Jackfruit has a stringy and firm texture that soaks up flavour extremely well, and is a brilliant substitute for meat in curries or in wraps drizzled with sauce. It is high in fibre and contains many vitamins.

JERK SEASONING
The ground spice seasoning element of the jerk marinating process includes fresh thyme, pimento and chilli. It can also be used to add a spicy kick to dishes.

LENTILS
Great source of protein and fibre and often used in soups, dhals and stews. Canned lentils are pre-cooked so are quicker to use.

LIME
We often use a squeeze of lime on a finished dish to balance the spice and sweetness.

MOLASSES
Usually used for sweets and cakes. In the process of extracting sugar from sugarcane, molasses is the dark, sweet syrupy by-product.

MUSHROOMS
This is the perfect ingredient if you're looking for a hearty dish as they have a firm texture and are brilliant at absorbing flavours. They are also high in fibre.

NUTMEG AND MACE
Used as a natural way to give a sweet and spiced kick to cakes, puddings and also drinks.

OKRA
Also known as lady fingers, it has a rubbery outer texture and sticky inside and is often used in soups. or stews. It can also be grilled or quickly fried for a crunchy bite.

PIMENTO
One of the most iconic ingredients of Jamaican cooking. Jerk chicken is cooked over pimento wood, and its unique smoky flavour makes jerk what it is. Whole pimento berries are used in recipes such as rice and peas, stews and meat dishes to give the recipe a flavaful aroma. The ground version is also known as allspice because its flavour is like a mix of cloves, cinnamon and nutmeg.

PLANTAIN
Part of the banana family, and comes in green, semi-ripe (with a mottled skin), or ripest and sweetest (with a black skin). Often fried or boiled – or even made into fries, as it has similar texture to potato.

PLANT-BASED MILK
There is now a large selection of plant-based milks to choose from: coconut, almond, oat and many more. We like to make our own, which led to us developing a plantain milk recipe (see page 30).

PUMPKIN
A sweet and starchy vegetable that is delicious in stews and can be used to thicken up soups and give them a creamy texture.

RICE
Basmati or long-grain, white or brown, whatever your preference this is a must-have ingredient in your cupboard for Caribbean cooking. It is the perfect side, either plain or as rice and peas.

ROOT VEGETABLES
Starchy vegetables such as cassava, yam, dasheen (taro), eddoes and sweet potatoes are most commonly used in soups and also simply boiled to be eaten as hard food.

SCOTCH BONNET
The famous chilli pepper is an iconic ingredient in Caribbean cooking. It's very hot so make sure you use with care. Remove the seeds and inner ribs before cooking if you want less spice, or chop it up or dash in the whole thing for extra spice.

SEA MOSS
Known for its many health benefits, it comes in a dried form and is first made into a gel by soaking and blending until smooth, before being added into smoothies and drinks.

SEITAN
Washing wheat flour dough removes the starch, leaving just the gluten behind, which is the main source of protein in wheat. It can be kneaded, seasoned and shaped to your preference, giving a solid element to your dish. It is often used as a meat substitute.

SORREL
The petals from the hibiscus plant can can be bought fresh from Afro-Caribbean food markets or dried from selected supermarkets. The dried form would first be soaked in water, creating a deep red colour and then usually sweetened with sugar, ginger and orange peel.

SPRING ONIONS
Used for multiple things such as a base to cooked down dishes, marinating meat, or in classic sauces and marinades. Also known as 'scallion' in the Caribbean.

POTATO
Potatoes or sweet potatoes are used often in soups and curries in the Caribbean, as it helps to fill your belly for longer and provides bulk to soups and stews to feed more people. The sweet potatoes in Jamaica tend to be yellow inside whereas orange is more common in the UK.

THYME
An essential herb for Caribbean cooking, either dashed into pans and sauteed, or floated to bring a delicious aroma to a soup mix. Sold in bunches of fresh or dried sprigs.

TOFU
Made from soy bean curd, it comes in many shapes and textures. In the Caribbean, the firm kind is often used as it is easier to cut up and it holds its shape when cooked. Pressing it removes excess water inside, which makes it easier to fry. It's also perfect to add to stews and curries.

TURMERIC
A strong yellow powdered spice used to bring the iconic colour to patties and Trini dhal. Be careful: it can easily stain your surfaces and clothes.

YAM
With a tough outer layer and starchy inside, it is often boiled in soups or cut up and cooked like fries.

Ingredients

Index

A

ackee 242
  ackee and cabbage with fried
    dumplings and plantain 28
  Caribbean breakfast muffin 26
  green banana, cornmeal dumplings,
    ackee, fried plantain, cabbage,
    callaloo flava bowl 65
  Ital breakfast platter 24
  special fried rice 205
almond milk
  sticky ginger cake 228
  yam and sweet potato chocolate
    pudding cake 232
almonds
  callaloo pesto pasta 70
  crunchy tropical granola 34
apples
  glow smoothie 32
  plantain and apple crumble 222
aubergines
  aubergines stuffed with spicy
    gungo peas 88
  Caribbean green seasoning curry 102
  jerk BBQ veggies 180
avocados 242
  callaloo pesto pasta 70
  chilli bean and avocado salad 214
  Ital breakfast platter 24
  jerk mushroom roti wraps 171
  spicy avocado, smashed plantain,
    bulgur wheat and peas, slaw,
    stew peas flava bowl 66
  stew pea dumpling taco 44

B

banana blossom 242
  spicy fried 'chicken' 57
bananas 242
  boost smoothie 32
  green banana, cornmeal dumplings,
    ackee, fried plantain, cabbage,
    callaloo flava bowl 65
  green banana curry 104
  hard-dough French toast
    with tropical fruits 20
  immune smoothie 32
bangers and mash, Caribbean 92
basil: callaloo pesto pasta 70
bay leaves 242
BBQ sauce, jerk 166

beans 242
  Caribbean chilli con carne 158
  chilli bean and avocado salad 214
  greens and beans 203
  lentil and bean stew 115
  lentil and bean stew, callaloo fritters, curry
    tofu and vegetables, greens and beans,
    bulgur wheat and peas flava bowl 67
  plantain and bean stew 120
black-eyed peas: coconut, black-eyed pea
  and sweet potato curry 107
blueberries, coconut pancakes with warm 18
bolognese, spicy 75
boost smoothie 32
bread
  garlic hard-dough bread 198
  hard-dough French toast
    with tropical fruits 20
  Ital breakfast platter 24
  jerk-spiced lentil burger 168
  plantain bread 226
breadfruit 242
breakfast muffins, Caribbean 26
breakfast platter, Ital 24
brioche: cauliflower burger with spicy
  mayo, slaw and mango chutney 91
broccoli
  brown stew broccoli 122
  greens and beans 203
  special fried rice 205
  sweet and sour tofu 79
  veggie dumpling pizza 94
brown stew broccoli 122
browning 242
bulgur wheat
  bulgur wheat and peas 204
  lentil and bean stew, callaloo fritters, curry
    tofu and vegetables, greens and beans,
    bulgur wheat and peas flava bowl 67
  spicy avocado, smashed plantain,
    bulgur wheat and peas, slaw, stew
    peas flava bowl 66
buns: Easter spice bun and cheese 234
burgers
  cauliflower burger with spicy mayo,
    slaw and mango chutney 91
  jerk-spiced lentil burger 168
buss up shut rotis 194–5
  chickpea and potato curry with 124
  jerk mushroom roti wraps 171
  meat-free kebabs 175
butter beans
  curry butter beans 114
  greens and beans 203

butternut squash
  green banana curry 104
  Ital pumpkin sip sip soup 138
  Ital stew 123
  jerk-spiced squash and callaloo
    Wellington 156
  Rasta pumpkin pasta 72
  red pea soup 141
  roasted butternut and chickpea salad
    with coconut mint dressing 211
  root vegetable stew with dumplings 127

C

cabbage
  ackee and cabbage with fried
    dumplings and plantain 28
  cauliflower burger with spicy mayo,
    slaw and mango chutney 91
  chilli bean and avocado salad 214
  curry tofu and vegetables 81
  green banana, cornmeal dumplings,
    ackee, fried plantain, cabbage,
    callaloo flava bowl 65
  Ital fruit salad 212
  jerk mushroom roti wraps 171
  mango coleslaw 184
  meat-free kebabs 175
cakes
  rum cake 227
  sticky ginger cake 228
  yam and sweet potato chocolate
    pudding cake 232
callaloo 242
  callaloo fritters 48
  callaloo patties 52
  callaloo pesto pasta 70
  Caribbean breakfast muffin 26
  green banana, cornmeal dumplings,
    ackee, fried plantain, cabbage,
    callaloo flava bowl 65
  Ital breakfast platter 24
  Ital stew, boiled yam and plantain,
    callaloo flava bowl 67
  jerk-spiced squash and callaloo
    Wellington 156
  lentil and bean stew, callaloo fritters, curry
    tofu and vegetables, greens and beans,
    bulgur wheat and peas flava bowl 67
  pepper pot soup 142
  sweet potato and callaloo pie 152
Caribbean bangers and mash 92
Caribbean breakfast muffin 26

Caribbean chilli con carne 158
Caribbean corn soup 139
Caribbean green seasoning curry 102
Caribbean-spiced jackfruit wraps with
   plum sauce 46
carrots
   Caribbean corn soup 139
   carrot juice 238
   creamy mushroom and okra stew 116
   curry butter beans 114
   glow smoothie 32
   green banana curry 104
   Ital pumpkin sip sip soup 138
   Ital stew 123
   jerk mushroom roti wraps 171
   lentil and bean stew 115
   mango coleslaw 184
   plantain and bean stew 120
   red pea soup 141
   root vegetable stew with dumplings 127
   vegan shepherd's pie 150
cauliflower 242
   cauliflower burger with spicy mayo,
      slaw and mango chutney 91
   jerk BBQ cauliflower
      'chicken wings' 172
cheese, vegan
   aubergines stuffed with spicy
      gungo peas 88
   Easter spice bun and cheese 234
   mac 'n' cheese 200
   plantain and spinach lasagne 144–5
   veggie dumpling pizza 94
cherries
   Easter spice bun and cheese 234
   rum cake 227
chia seeds
   detox smoothie 32
   lentil nut roast 153
'chicken', spicy fried 57
chickpeas
   chickpea and potato curry with buss
      up shut roti 124
   curried chickpea plantain boat 110
   green banana curry 104
   plantain hummus 42
   roasted butternut and chickpea salad
      with coconut mint dressing 211
   spicy chickpea mayo 86
   sweet potato and chickpea peanut
      stew with jollof rice 109
   vegan shepherd's pie 150
chilli jam 215
   yam fries with 208
chillies
   Caribbean chilli con carne 158
   chilli bean and avocado salad 214
   chilli jam 215
   grilled chilli herb corn 181
   see also scotch bonnet peppers
chocolate
   plantain choc chip cookies 224
   yam and sweet potato chocolate
      pudding cake 232
cinnamon: warm-spiced cornmeal
   porridge 31

coconut 242
   coconut pancakes with warm
      blueberries 18
   crunchy tropical granola 34
   fresh coconut milk 30
   special fried rice 205
coconut cream: tomato and coconut
   pasta 78
coconut milk 242
   bulgur wheat and peas 204
   Caribbean corn soup 139
   Caribbean green seasoning curry 102
   carrot juice 238
   cauliflower burger with spicy mayo,
      slaw and mango chutney 91
   coconut, black-eyed pea and sweet
      potato curry 107
   coconut pancakes with warm
      blueberries 18
   creamy mushroom and okra stew 116
   curried chickpea plantain boat 110
   curry jackfruit 106
   curry tofu and vegetables 81
   fresh coconut milk 30
   green banana curry 104
   Guinness punch 239
   Irish moss 240
   Ital breakfast platter 24
   Ital pelau rice 202
   Ital stew 123
   jackfruit rundown 128
   jerk BBQ cauliflower 'chicken wings' 172
   pepper pot soup 142
   Rasta pumpkin pasta 72
   red pea soup 141
   spicy coconut ramen 82
   spicy fried 'chicken' 57
   stew pea dumpling taco 44
   tomato and coconut pasta 78
   vegan shepherd's pie 150
   warm-spiced cornmeal porridge 31
coconut water: immune smoothie 32
coconut yoghurt
   coconut mint dressing 211
   Rasta pumpkin pasta 72
coleslaw, mango 184
condensed milk 242
   Irish moss 240
   soursop juice 235
cookies, plantain choc chip 224
coriander 242
corn
   Caribbean corn soup 139
   corn fritters 54
   grilled chilli herb corn 181
   mango coleslaw 184
cornmeal 243
   green banana, cornmeal dumplings,
      ackee, fried plantain, cabbage,
      callaloo flava bowl 65
   warm-spiced cornmeal porridge 31
courgettes
   jerk BBQ veggies 180
   veggie dumpling pizza 94
creamy mushroom and okra stew 116
crumble, plantain and apple 222

crunchy tropical granola 34
cucumber
   Caribbean-spiced jackfruit wraps
      with plum sauce 46
   detox smoothie 32
   immune smoothie 32
   Ital fruit salad 212
curry 243
   Caribbean green seasoning curry 102
   chickpea and potato curry with buss
      up shut roti 124
   coconut, black-eyed pea and sweet
      potato curry 107
   curried chickpea plantain boat 110
   curry butter beans 114
   curry jackfruit 106
   curry tofu and vegetables 81
   green banana curry 104
   lentil and bean stew, callaloo fritters,
      curry tofu and vegetables, greens
      and beans, bulgur wheat and peas
      flava bowl 67

D
dasheen
   Ital pumpkin sip sip soup 138
   red pea soup 141
dates: plantain milk 30
detox smoothie 32
dhal: Trini split pea dhal with spinach
   and okra 118
dressing, coconut mint 211
dried fruit
   Easter spice bun and cheese 234
   lentil nut roast 153
   rum cake 227
drinks
   boost smoothie 32
   detox smoothie 32
   glow smoothie 32
   Guinness punch 239
   immune smoothie 32
   Irish moss 240
   Ital smoothies 32
   lemongrass tea 35
   mint tea 35
   sorrel punch 237
   soursop juice 235
dumplings
   ackee and cabbage with fried
      dumplings and plantain 28
   green banana, cornmeal dumplings,
      ackee, fried plantain, cabbage,
      callaloo flava bowl 65
   root vegetable stew
      with dumplings 127
   stew pea dumpling taco 44
   veggie dumpling pizza 94

E
Easter spice bun and cheese 234
escovitch tofish 147

F

flava bowls 64–7
    green banana, cornmeal dumplings,
        ackee, fried plantain, cabbage,
        callaloo flava bowl 65
    Ital stew, boiled yam and plantain,
        callaloo flava bowl 67
    lentil and bean stew,
        callaloo fritters, curry tofu
        and vegetables, greens and
        beans, bulgur wheat and
        peas flava bowl 67
    spicy avocado, smashed plantain,
        bulgur wheat and peas, slaw, stew
        peas flava bowl 66
flaxseeds 243
French toast
    hard-dough French toast
        with tropical fruits 20
    Ital breakfast platter 24
fries, yam 208
fritters
    callaloo fritters 48
    corn fritters 54
    lentil and bean stew,
        callaloo fritters, curry tofu
        and vegetables, greens and
        beans, bulgur wheat and
        peas flava bowl 67
fruit 243
    hard-dough French toast
        with tropical fruits 20
    Ital fruit salad 212
    jerk BBQ fruit platter 187
    see also dried fruit and individual
        types of fruit

G

garlic
    ackee and cabbage with fried
        dumplings and plantain 28
    callaloo patties 52
    callaloo pesto pasta 70
    curry jackfruit 106
    garlic hard-dough bread 198
    green banana curry 104
    greens and beans 203
    Ital pumpkin sip sip soup 138
    jerk BBQ roast 177
    plantain hummus 42
    Rasta pumpkin pasta 72
    stew pea dumpling taco 44
    sweet and sour tofu 79
    tomato and coconut pasta 78
ginger 243
    glow smoothie 32
    sticky ginger cake 228
glacé cherries
    Easter spice bun and cheese 234
    rum cake 227
glaze, miso 82
glow smoothie 32
granola, crunchy tropical 34

green bananas 242
    green banana, cornmeal
        dumplings, ackee,
        fried plantain, cabbage,
        callaloo flava bowl 65
    green banana curry 104
green beans
    Caribbean green seasoning
        curry 102
    greens and beans 203
green seasoning 102, 243
    Ital pelau rice 202
greens
    greens and beans 203
    Ital stew 123
    lentil and bean stew,
        callaloo fritters, curry tofu
        and vegetables, greens and
        beans, bulgur wheat and
        peas flava bowl 67
guava jam: Ital fruit salad 212
Guinness
    Easter spice bun and
        cheese 234
    Guinness punch 239
    Irish moss 240
gungo peas
    aubergines stuffed with spicy
        gungo peas 88
    Ital pelau rice 202

H

hard-dough French toast
    with tropical fruits 20
herbs: grilled chilli herb corn 181
hoisin sauce:
    Caribbean-spiced jackfruit
        wraps with plum sauce 46
hummus, plantain 42

I

immune smoothie 32
ingredients 242–4
Irish moss 240
Ital breakfast platter 24
Ital fruit salad 212
Ital pelau rice 202
Ital pumpkin sip sip soup 138
Ital smoothies 32
Ital stew 123
    Ital stew, boiled yam and plantain,
        callaloo flava bowl 67

J

jackfruit 243
    Caribbean-spiced jackfruit
        wrapswith plum sauce 46
    curry jackfruit 106
    jackfruit rundown 128
jam, chilli 215

jerk
    Caribbean bangers and mash 92
    jerk BBQ sauce 166
    jerk mushroom roti wraps 171
    jerk seasoning 166, 243
    jerk-spiced lentil burger 168
    jerk-spiced squash and callaloo
        Wellington 156
    Rasta pumpkin pasta 72
jerk BBQ sauce 166
    jerk BBQ cauliflower 'chicken wings' 172
    jerk BBQ veggies 180
    jerk tofu 178
jerk seasoning 166, 243
    jerk BBQ fruit platter 187
    jerk BBQ roast 177
    jerk BBQ veggies 180
    jerk tofu 178
jollof rice, sweet potato and chickpea
    peanut stew with 109
juices
    carrot juice 238
    soursop juice 235

K

kale: sweet potato and chickpea
    peanut stew with jollof rice 109
kebabs, meat-free 175
kidney beans
    bulgur wheat and peas 204
    plantain and bean stew 120
    red pea soup 141
    stew pea dumpling taco 44
kiwi fruit
    detox smoothie 32
    Ital fruit salad 212

L

lasagne, plantain and spinach 144–5
lemongrass tea 35
lentils 243
    Ital stew 123
    jerk-spiced lentil burger 168
    lentil and bean stew 115
    lentil and bean stew,
        callaloo fritters, curry tofu
        and vegetables, greens and
        beans, bulgur wheat and peas
        flava bowl 67
    lentil nut roast 153
    vegan shepherd's pie 150
lettuce
    Ital fruit salad 212
    meat-free kebabs 175
    roasted butternut and chickpea
        salad with coconut mint dressing 211
limes 243

M

mac 'n' cheese 200

Index

mango
    boost smoothie 32
    crunchy tropical granola 34
    hard-dough French toast with
       tropical fruits 20
    jerk BBQ fruit platter 187
    mango chilli sauce 215
    mango coleslaw 184
mango chutney, cauliflower burger
  with spicy mayo, slaw and 91
mayo, vegan
    jerk mushroom roti wraps 171
    mango coleslaw 184
    spicy chickpea mayo 86
    spicy mayo 91
    sweet potato salad 185
meat-free kebabs 175
milks, plant-based 243
    fresh coconut milk 30
    mac 'n' cheese 200
    plantain milk 30
mince, meat-free
    Caribbean chilli con carne 158
    giant patty 154
    no-bully-beef stew 129
    plantain and spinach lasagne 144–5
    spicy bolognese 75
mint
    coconut mint dressing 211
    mint tea 35
miso glaze 82
muffins, Caribbean breakfast 26
mushrooms 243
    brown stew broccoli 122
    creamy mushroom and
       okra stew 116
    giant patty 154
    Ital breakfast platter 24
    jerk BBQ veggies 180
    jerk mushroom roti wraps 171
    jerk-spiced lentil burger 168
    jerk-spiced squash and callaloo
       Wellington 156
    lentil nut roast 153
    mushroom pepper steak 85
    special fried rice 205
    spicy bolognese 75
    spicy coconut ramen 82

N

no-bully-beef stew 129
noodles: spicy coconut ramen 82
nuts
    lentil nut roast 153
    spiced pepper nuts 136

O

oat milk:
  warm-spiced cornmeal porridge 31
oats
    crunchy tropical granola 34
    jerk-spiced lentil burger 168

okra 243
    creamy mushroom and okra stew 116
    pepper pot soup 142
    Trini split pea dhal with spinach
       and okra 118
    veggie dumpling pizza 94
orange juice: sorrel punch 237
oyster mushrooms: spicy coconut ramen 82

P

pak choi: spicy coconut ramen 82
pancakes: coconut pancakes
  with warm blueberries 18
papaya
    crunchy tropical granola 34
    hard-dough French toast with tropical
      fruits 20
    Ital fruit salad 212
passion fruit
    hard-dough French toast with tropical
      fruits 20
    Ital fruit salad 212
pasta
    callaloo pesto pasta 70
    mac 'n' cheese 200
    plantain and spinach lasagne 144–5
    Rasta pumpkin pasta 72
    spicy bolognese 75
    tomato and coconut pasta 78
patties
    callaloo patties 52
    giant patty 154
peaches: jerk BBQ fruit platter 187
peanut butter: sweet potato and chickpea
  peanut stew with jollof rice 109
peas 242
    bulgur wheat and peas 204
    lentil and bean stew, callaloo fritters,
      curry tofu and vegetables, greens
      and beans, bulgur wheat and peas
      flava bowl 67
    spicy avocado, smashed plantain,
      bulgur wheat and peas, slaw, stew
      peas flava bowl 66
    sweet potato and callaloo pie 152
    vegan shepherd's pie 150
pepper pot soup 142
peppers
    aubergines stuffed with spicy
      gungo peas 88
    brown stew broccoli 122
    callaloo fritters 48
    Caribbean breakfast muffin 26
    Caribbean chilli con carne 158
    Caribbean green seasoning curry 102
    chilli bean and avocado salad 214
    chilli jam 215
    curry butter beans 114
    curry tofu and vegetables 81
    escovitch tofish 147
    green banana curry 104
    Ital pelau rice 202
    jackfruit rundown 128
    jerk BBQ veggies 180

lentil nut roast 153
mango chilli sauce 215
mushroom pepper steak 85
no-bully-beef stew 129
Rasta pumpkin pasta 72
roasted butternut and chickpea salad
  with coconut mint dressing 211
scotch bonnet sauce 215
special fried rice 205
sweet and sour tofu 79
sweet potato and callaloo pie 152
sweet potato and chickpea peanut
  stew with jollof rice 109
sweet potato salad 185
veggie dumpling pizza 94
pesto: callaloo pesto pasta 70
pies
    sweet potato and callaloo pie 152
    vegan shepherd's pie 150
pimento 243
pineapple
    boost smoothie 32
    glow smoothie 32
    hard-dough French toast
      with tropical fruits 20
    Ital fruit salad 212
    jerk BBQ fruit platter 187
    sweet and sour tofu 79
pineapple juice
    glow smoothie 32
    sorrel punch 237
pizza, veggie dumpling 94
plantain 243
    ackee and cabbage with fried
      dumplings and plantain 28
    Caribbean bangers and mash 92
    Caribbean breakfast muffin 26
    crunchy tropical granola 34
    curried chickpea plantain boat 110
    green banana, cornmeal dumplings,
      ackee, fried plantain, cabbage,
      callaloo flava bowl 65
    Ital breakfast platter 24
    Ital stew 123
    Ital stew, boiled yam and plantain,
      callaloo flava bowl 67
    meat-free kebabs 175
    plantain and apple crumble 222
    plantain and bean stew 120
    plantain and spinach lasagne 144–5
    plantain bread 226
    plantain choc chip cookies 224
    plantain hummus 42
    plantain milk 30
    spicy avocado, smashed
      plantain, bulgur wheat
      and peas, slaw, stew peas
      flava bowl 66
platters
    Ital breakfast platter 24
    jerk BBQ fruit platter 187
plums
    Caribbean-spiced jackfruit wraps
      with plum sauce 46
    jerk BBQ fruit platter 187
porridge, warm-spiced cornmeal 31

Index

Portobello mushrooms
    jerk BBQ veggies 180
    jerk mushroom roti wraps 171
    mushroom pepper steak 85
potatoes 244
    chickpea and potato curry with buss
      up shut roti 124
    creamy mushroom and okra stew 116
    curry jackfruit 106
    pepper pot soup 142
    rum-roasted potatoes 207
    spicy fried 'chicken' 57
    vegan shepherd's pie 150
puff pastry: jerk-spiced squash
  and callaloo Wellington 156
pumpkin 243
    Caribbean corn soup 139
    green banana curry 104
    Ital pumpkin sip sip soup 138
    Ital stew 123
    pepper pot soup 142
    Rasta pumpkin pasta 72
    red pea soup 141
    root vegetable stew
      with dumplings 127
pumpkin seeds: immune smoothie 32
punch
    Guinness punch 239
    sorrel punch 237

R

raisins: plantain bread 226
ramen, spicy coconut 82
Rasta pumpkin pasta 72
red pea soup 141
rice 243
    Ital pelau rice 202
    special fried rice 205
    sweet potato and chickpea peanut
      stew with jollof rice 109
root vegetables 244
    root vegetable stew with dumplings 127
rotis, buss up shut 194–5
    chickpea and potato curry with 124
    jerk mushroom roti wraps 171
rum
    carrot juice 238
    Guinness punch 239
    Irish moss 240
    rum cake 227
    rum-roasted potatoes 207
    sorrel punch 237
rundown, jackfruit 128

S

salads
    cauliflower burger with spicy mayo,
      slaw and mango chutney 91
    chilli bean and avocado salad 214
    Ital fruit salad 212
    jerk mushroom roti wraps 171
    mango coleslaw 184

roasted butternut and chickpea salad
  with coconut mint dressing 211
spicy avocado, smashed plantain,
  bulgur wheat and peas, slaw, stew
  peas flava bowl 66
sweet potato salad 185
sauces 215
sausages:
  Caribbean bangers and mash 92
scotch bonnet peppers 244
    ackee and cabbage with fried
      dumplings and plantain 28
    aubergines stuffed with spicy
      gungo peas 88
    brown stew broccoli 122
    callaloo fritters 48
    callaloo patties 52
    callaloo pesto pasta 70
    Caribbean bangers and mash 92
    Caribbean chilli con carne 158
    Caribbean corn soup 139
    Caribbean-spiced jackfruit wraps with
      plum sauce 46
    cauliflower burger with spicy mayo,
      slaw and mango chutney 91
    chickpea and potato curry with buss
      up shut roti 124
    chilli jam 215
    coconut, black-eyed pea and sweet
      potato curry 107
    corn fritters 54
    giant patty 154
    green banana, cornmeal dumplings,
      ackee, fried plantain, cabbage,
      callaloo flava bowl 65
    green banana curry 104
    greens and beans 203
    grilled chilli herb corn 181
    Ital breakfast platter 24
    Ital pelau rice 202
    Ital pumpkin sip sip soup 138
    jackfruit rundown 128
    jerk BBQ roast 177
    lentil and bean stew 115
    lentil nut roast 153
    mac 'n' cheese 200
    mango chilli sauce 215
    meat-free kebabs 175
    pepper pot soup 142
    plantain and bean stew 120
    plantain and spinach lasagne 144–5
    plantain hummus 42
    Rasta pumpkin pasta 72
    red pea soup 141
    root vegetable stew with dumplings 127
    rum-roasted potatoes 207
    scotch bonnet sauce 215
    special fried rice 205
    spiced pepper nuts 136
    spicy bolognese 75
    stew pea dumpling taco 44
    sweet potato and callaloo pie 152
    sweet potato and chickpea peanut
      stew with jollof rice 109
    sweet potato salad 185
    tomato and coconut pasta 78

Trini split pea dhal with spinach
  and okra 118
veggie dumpling pizza 94
yam fries with scotch bonnet
  sauce or chilli jam 208
sea moss 244
    Irish moss 240
    sea moss gel 240
seasonings 242
    green seasoning 102
    jerk seasoning 166
seitan 244
shepherd's pie, vegan 150
sides 188–215
slaws
    cauliflower burger with
      spicy mayo, slaw and
      mango chutney 91
    jerk mushroom roti wraps 171
    mango coleslaw 184
    spicy avocado, smashed
      plantain, bulgur wheat
      and peas, slaw, stew peas
      flava bowl 66
smoothies
    boost smoothie 32
    detox smoothie 32
    glow smoothie 32
    immune smoothie 32
    Ital smoothies 32
snacks 36–57
sorrel 244
    sorrel punch 237
soups
    Caribbean corn soup 139
    Ital pumpkin sip sip soup 138
    pepper pot soup 142
    red pea soup 141
soursop juice 235
spaghetti: callaloo pesto pasta 70
special fried rice 205
spiced pepper nuts 136
spicy avocado, smashed plantain,
  bulgur wheat and peas, slaw,
  stew peas flava bowl 66
spicy bolognese 75
spicy chickpea mayo 86
spicy coconut ramen 82
spicy fried 'chicken' 57
spinach
    ackee and cabbage with fried
      dumplings and plantain 28
    callaloo pesto pasta 70
    immune smoothie 32
    plantain and spinach
      lasagne 144–5
    Trini split pea dhal with spinach
      and okra 118
spirulina: immune smoothie 32
split peas: Trini split pea dhal
  with spinach and okra 118
spring greens
    greens and beans 203
    Ital pumpkin sip sip soup 138
    red pea soup 141
spring onions 244

squash
 jerk-spiced squash and callaloo
  Wellington 156
 Rasta pumpkin pasta 72
 red pea soup 141
 roasted butternut and chickpea salad
  with coconut mint dressing 211
stew peas
 spicy avocado, smashed plantain,
  bulgur wheat and peas, slaw, stew
  peas flava bowl 66
 stew pea dumpling taco 44
stews
 brown stew broccoli 122
 creamy mushroom and okra stew 116
 Ital stew 123
 Ital stew, boiled yam and plantain,
  callaloo flava bowl 67
 lentil and bean stew 115
 lentil and bean stew, callaloo fritters,
  curry tofu and vegetables, greens
  and beans, bulgur wheat and peas
  flava bowl 67
 no-bully-beef stew 129
 plantain and bean stew 120
 root vegetable stew with dumplings 127
 sweet potato and chickpea peanut
  stew with jollof rice 109
sticky ginger cake 228
stuffing mix: lentil nut roast 153
sweet and sour tofu 79
sweet potatoes
 baked sweet potatoes with spicy
  chickpea mayo 86
 coconut, black-eyed pea and sweet
  potato curry 107
 pepper pot soup 142
 sweet potato and callaloo pie 152
 sweet potato and chickpea peanut
  stew with jollof rice 109
 sweet potato salad 185
 yam and sweet potato chocolate
  pudding cake 232
sweetcorn
 Caribbean corn soup 139
 chilli bean and avocado salad 214
 corn fritters 54
 grilled chilli herb corn 181
 Ital pumpkin sip sip soup 138
 jerk mushroom roti wraps 171
 mango coleslaw 184
 no-bully-beef stew 129
 roasted butternut and chickpea salad
  with coconut mint dressing 211
 sweet potato salad 185

toast
 hard-dough French toast
  with tropical fruits 20
 Ital breakfast platter 24
tofu 244
 curry tofu and vegetables 81
 escovitch tofish 147
 jerk tofu 178
 lentil and bean stew, callaloo fritters,
  curry tofu and vegetables, greens
  and beans, bulgur wheat and peas
  flava bowl 67
 spicy coconut ramen 82
 sweet and sour tofu 79
tomato ketchup: jerk BBQ sauce 166
tomatoes
 aubergines stuffed with spicy gungo
  peas 88
 callaloo fritters 48
 callaloo pesto pasta 70
 Caribbean chilli con carne 158
 chilli bean and avocado salad 214
 green banana, cornmeal dumplings,
  ackee, fried plantain, cabbage,
  callaloo flava bowl 65
 green banana curry 104
 Ital breakfast platter 24
 Ital stew 123
 lentil and bean stew 115
 meat-free kebabs 175
 plantain and bean stew 120
 plantain and spinach lasagne 144–5
 spicy avocado, smashed plantain,
  bulgur wheat and peas, slaw, stew
  peas flava bowl 66
 spicy bolognese 75
 stew pea dumpling taco 44
 sweet potato and chickpea peanut
  stew with jollof rice 109
 tomato and coconut pasta 78
 vegan shepherd's pie 150
 veggie dumpling pizza 94
tortilla wraps: Caribbean-spiced jackfruit
 wraps with plum sauce 46
Trini split pea dhal with spinach and okra 118
tropical fruits, hard-dough French toast
 with 20
tropical granola, crunchy 34
turmeric 244
 glow smoothie 32
 Trini split pea dhal with spinach
  and okra 118

W

walnuts: callaloo pesto pasta 70
warm-spiced cornmeal porridge 31
watermelon
 detox smoothie 32
 jerk BBQ fruit platter 187
Wellington, jerk-spiced squash
 and callaloo 156
wine
 jerk BBQ roast 177
 rum cake 227
 sorrel punch 237
wraps
 Caribbean-spiced jackfruit wraps
  with plum sauce 46
 jerk mushroom roti wraps 171

Y

yams 244
 Ital pumpkin sip sip soup 138
 Ital stew, boiled yam and plantain,
  callaloo flava bowl 67
 pepper pot soup 142
 red pea soup 141
 root vegetable stew with dumplings 127
 yam and sweet potato chocolate
  pudding cake 232
 yam fries with scotch bonnet sauce
  or chilli jam 208
yoghurt
 coconut mint dressing 211
 Rasta pumpkin pasta 72

T

tacos, stew pea dumpling 44
tahini: plantain hummus 42
tea
 lemongrass tea 35
 mint tea 35
tenderstem broccoli:
 greens and beans 203

V

vegan milks 30
vegan shepherd's pie 150
vegetables 244
 curry tofu and vegetables 81
 jerk BBQ veggies 180
 lentil and bean stew, callaloo fritters, curry
  tofu and vegetables, greens and beans,
  bulgur wheat and peas flava bowl 67
 root vegetable stew with dumplings 127
veggie dumpling pizza 94

Index

Acknowledgements

Jesus, I thank you for the incredible doors you are opening for us. Special thanks go to my wonderful family: my wife, Natalie, whose support and prayers lift me every day, my daughters Rebecca-Louise and Leia, who are my pride, joy, and the reason I do what I do. I love you all so much. Becoming a father has been undoubtedly the proudest moment of my life. And to have them in this book is a memory that can never be erased.

My right-hand man, my brother, Shaun, who continues to push me to do my best. And to stay relatively trim when so much food is around us! We've come a long way with Original Flava, and our hard work and dedication to it keeps us grounded to be the very best in the game! LET'S GO!

My ever-supportive parents, who have been my cheerleaders since day one, having my back in every area of life. Thank you Mum and Dad, and our elder brother, Lewis, too. Nanny Mitchell, my friend and rock! Thank you for believing in Original Flava and having the patience to endure our shenanigans during the early stages of the journey! Your love and spirit are unmatched.

Team Original Flava, your support helps make Original Flava what it is today, and what it will become.

On behalf of both of us, we would like to thank the awesome people at Bloomsbury Publishing for trusting us, believing in two brothers from South London and giving us free rein to make this book our own. Also, Matt Russell for putting up with us again and taking some great photos! Love you man. Nena and the food styling team, and the designers, Evi, Nicole and Susan! This all wouldn't have been possible without you. THANK YOU!

Last but not least, thank you to the FLAVA FAMILY, from our followers on social media to anyone who has bought our books, come to an Original Flava supperclub or just showed us love. We really appreciate you.

— Craig

Firstly, I would like to thank my Lord and saviour Jesus Christ for giving me the gift of cooking and sharing it with the world. This opportunity would not have been possible without him. I pray that the Lord continues to bless us and keep us grounded. Amen.

Massive thank you to my fiancée, Brenda, for giving me the time and space to work on Original Flava and this book. There have been some long nights and days; thank you for always supporting my passion and for looking after our son. Love you so much.

To my son, Leo, I love you very much. You are always looking at our previous cookbook with a big smile and saying 'Daddy'. Now you're in this book! You are a smart and caring young boy and I'm so proud of you. You can be anything you want to be! I can see you love cooking already; I'll make sure you're a better cook than me!

Big thank you to my brother, my business partner, my best friend, Craig, for being on this journey with me. Thank you for believing in me! We are building something great and there's more to come. We are going to leave a legacy for our kids to be proud of.

I would also like to thank our Nan, Nanny Mitchell, for being an awesome support to us. We used her kitchen to start Original Flava back in 2016. Nan is the rock of the family and the rock of Original Flava too! Thank you, Nanny, for the sacrifices you've made for us.

Massive love and thanks to Mum and Dad, for always being there for me when I needed them and being supportive in our Original Flava journey and teaching me the meaning of hard work and discipline. A big thank to my older brother Lewis, for helping out where he can.

Thank you to the FLAVA TEAM, who have contributed so much to get us to where we are today. Also, to my friends who have seen our journey from the start and have always been so supportive.

I would like to give a final, special thank you to our followers, who are like our family and have been with us through thick and thin. Thank you for inspiring us to keep growing and improving. This book is for you guys!

— Shaun

BLOOMSBURY PUBLISHING
Bloomsbury Publishing Plc
50 Bedford Square, London, WC1B 3DP, UK
29 Earlsfort Terrace, Dublin 2, Ireland

First published in Great Britain 2022

A catalogue record for this book is available from the
British Library.

Library of Congress Cataloguing-in-Publication data has
been applied for.

ISBN: HB: 978-1-5266-3187-9
eBook: 978-1-5266-3186-2

10 9 8 7 6 5 4 3 2 1

Designer: Evi-O.Studio | Evi O., Susan Le & Nicole Ho
Photographer: Matt Russell
Food Stylists: Nena Foster and Joanna Jackson
Prop Stylist: Wei Tang
Indexer: Vanessa Bird

Printed and bound in China by C&C Offset Printing Co., Ltd

Bloomsbury Publishing Plc makes every effort to ensure
that the papers used in the manufacture of our books are
natural, recyclable products made from wood grown in well-
managed forests. Our manufacturing processes conform
to the environmental regulations of the country of origin.

To find out more about our authors and books visit
www.bloomsbury.com and sign up for our newsletters.